Praise for *Social Media 101*

"Dismissing social media is not an option, but neither is recruiting a small army of consultants to move your business forward. If you need a crisp view of what's relevant and how to implement what's measurable and meaningful *today* do not miss *Social Media 101*. Chris Brogan has clearly established himself as the "Social Media Compass" for the rest of us. By the time you finish reading this sentence, there's something new to tweet about, but you can count on Chris to keep you headed in the right direction."

—Beth Dockins
Director, Customer Service, Scotts

"Social media is a new and fascinating playground for the complexities of human nature. Chris Brogan understands social media because he puts in the time—observing, understanding, and most importantly, taking action in ways that work."

—Brian Clark
Owner/Publisher of Copyblogger.com

"*Social Media 101* is packed full of the kind of actionable information I wish I'd had starting out in the game."

—Darren Rowse
Publisher of Problogger.net

"It's terrific to see Chris Brogan capturing so many of his thoughts on social media in one resource. He's a person who I follow just for that reason. He offers clever insights and is always at the front of the learning curve."

—Ferg Devins
Chief Public Affairs Officer, Molson Coors Canada

"Don't know where to start with social media? Chris Brogan takes your hand and guides you through—with a smile."

—Jennifer Cisney
Kodak Chief Blogger and Social Media Manager

Social Media

101

Tactics and Tips to Develop Your Business Online

Chris Brogan

WILEY

John Wiley & Sons, Inc.

Published by John Wiley & Sons, Inc., Hoboken, New Jersey.
Published simultaneously in Canada.

For general information on our other products and services or for technical support, please
contact our Customer Care Department within the United States at (800) 762-2974,
outside the United States at (317) 572-3993 or fax (317) 572-4002.

Wiley also publishes its books in a variety of electronic formats. Some content that
appears in print may not be available in electronic books. For more information about
Wiley products, visit our web site at www.wiley.com.

Library of Congress Cataloging-in-Publication Data:
Brogan, Chris.
   Social media 101 : tactics and tips to develop your business online / by Chris Brogan.
      p. cm.
   Includes bibliographical references and index.
   ISBN 978-0-470-56341-0 (cloth : alk. paper)
  1. Internet marketing.   2. Social media—Economic aspects.   3. Customer
relations—Management.   4. Information technology—Management.   I. Title.
   HF5415.1265.B758 2010
   658.8'72—dc22
                                       2009051244

Printed in the United States of America
10 9 8 7 6 5 4 3 2 1

Contents

To my mom and dad, Diane and Steve Brogan, who did a LOT of the editing on this book, and who are helping me run my business. Who'd have ever thunk it?

Acknowledgments

Thanks to Matt Holt and Shannon Vargo from Wiley, for every little bit of kindness along the way, and an extra scoop to Shannon for catching my random tweet and turning it into a book idea.

Introduction: Why in the World Should You Care?

You might be reading this in a bookstore or in an online preview, and you might be wondering why you should bother. Books about social media are as ubiquitous as books about golf, as common as hip-hop songs using Auto-Tune. The world needs another social media book like it needs another new reality TV show.

If I promise that this is a bit different than other social media books, would that be enough to get you to keep reading?

When Julien Smith and I wrote *Trust Agents,* a lot of people thought we were going to write a book about social media. It's often reviewed as a book about social media, and yet it's not. Not really. It's a book about how people can earn trust using many factors, including the use of online tools.

Because I didn't write the book you expected, I thought I'd present you with this book. *This* book is about social media.

Social media tools aren't something new anymore. They might not be used by you and your company just yet, but they are everywhere in the marketplace. Your competitors are using them. Your customers are almost definitely using social media tools.

I've written this book in the hope that it's useful to both existing practitioners and people looking for a solid starting point.

More likely than not, this book is something you've bought for the person in the office who needs to "get it." *This* book will help you solve that one.

Repetition abounds in this book. I frequently talk about the same tools in slightly different ways. This is intentional. I'm presenting this information in such a way that any one piece of it can stand on its own. We called this "Give your ideas handles" in *Trust Agents,* and the plan works here, too. By the end of this book, you'll know exactly how I feel about things like Twitter, Facebook, blogging, and all the rest of it.

One final note before we dig in: This book is a collection of several posts that originally appeared at www.chrisbrogan .com. You *could* get this book (in a very raw form) from my blog for free (minus all my updates and edits). I teased best-selling author and entrepreneur Guy Kawasaki about this when he published his book, *Reality Bites,* which is an excellent collection of Guy's wisdom. I'm saying this because now I'm going to have to listen to Guy (who keynotes on *many* stages each year) tease me for doing the same kind of thing.

I promise this: If you've bought the book, there will likely be some new things you take away from it. It's *packed* with info.

Let's begin.

1

Above All Else—People

Have you had a good conversation lately? What do you remember about it? Who do you enjoy having conversations with?

Conversations require people, and the purpose of social media is to empower and enable conversations digitally. Blogging, podcasting, video blogging, and all the various social networks we use are all geared toward one thing: giving us a way to reach out and connect. With that in mind, let's start this out right and consider *people*. Let's think about people from *their* perspective.

What follows are some ideas for engaging, respecting, and appreciating the people who will interact with your social media.

PEOPLE LIKE TO BE ENGAGED

Imagine there is a choice (because there is). You can either speak *at* people or you can speak *with* people. One assumes that the other person or persons will have an opportunity to say something back at some point. Which scenario would you prefer: one where you're sitting idly while someone goes on and on, or one where you're just as important to things as the person who started the conversation? I'm going to say the latter.

One way to engage people is to ask a question. How did I start this topic? I asked a question that put you back in *your* head.

Another way is to encourage people to take part in the activities. Don't let them be the audience. *Audience* is a passive term. Think of ways to get people into the story. Can you come up with a way that they can contribute? Are there ways you can encourage follow-on activity in their world?

PEOPLE ARE BUSY

Respect people's time when creating your media. Don't ramble in a podcast just because you can. My wife, Katrina, always says, "Editing is good manners." She means that by being respectful of people's time, you win their appreciation.

One way to do this is to lead with your lead. Tell the *best* stuff up front in your blog post or your podcast. Give people a rundown of where you're going as early as you can. Lots of great media makers script their productions, outline their blog posts, and otherwise use systems to stay on point.

Make sure you provide many ways to subscribe to your media. Posting an RSS link isn't really going far enough unless you show people how to subscribe in the way *they* want it. If it's a blog, show them how to get it by e-mail, if that's their reading choice. If it's a video blog, show your audience how they can stay up-to-date with your media. Ask whether you can notify them of special shows you don't want them to miss, perhaps by sending an e-mail. If they agree, use that method *sparingly*

Don't make every show a must-see show. Make the best ones a must-see.

PEOPLE LIKE TO BE APPRECIATED

You're not doing this for yourself (unless you are). The notion is that you're out there trying to build a relationship with an audience. If you're in business, you're establishing brand, or talking about a product, or pitching something in a more human, two-way method. If you're an individual, you're building reputation, sharing information with like-minded sources. In all these cases, it's two-way, and the people on the other side want to know you respect that.

Stop by other people's sites now and again. Leave comments. Point the occasional blog post or podcast out toward the folks who spend their time with you. Go further than a blogroll. Drive awareness. Build traffic.

A while back, I promoted musician Matthew Ebel's project, www.virtualhotwings.com, which allowed fans of his music to buy some very special tracks that weren't otherwise collected or available. But further, the project sent out updates for new tracks that purchasers of the original project received free for having paid for the project the first time. That kind of follow-on appreciation makes lifelong fans from people interested in your media.

As a producer of a blog or a podcast or other media, consider ways to give people something more for the attention they're spending on you. Think of ways to make special offers for free things to acknowledge that someone's a fan of your work, or better still, find ways to promote the people in your audience as the true stars in your social media system. Make it every bit as much about them as it is about your relationship with them.

MAKE PEOPLE THE EXPERTS

Finally, seek ways to tap into people's expertise. The point behind unconferences like PodCamp[1] is that the intelligence and brainpower in the audience is almost always going to be greater than what would normally be up on a stage at a traditional conference. To that end, seek ways to tap your audience for their expertise. Ask them to tell you about things. Find out what *they* know. (You already know what *you* know.)

That's why I end every post with a question. It's a way to prompt for interaction, but it's also a way to learn from the people who spend time with me. I learned a long time ago that the folks spending time with me know more than me in the aggregate. I can start a great conversation, but they always have the better ideas in sum. So ask for it. Seek information. Learn from them.

Besides, people love giving their opinions. It's a great way to give them the chance to do so.

Have you tried this before? How did it work for you?

---

[1]http://podcamp.org/

What Social Media Does Best

If you're still looking for the best ways to explain to senior management or your team or your coworkers or your spouse what social media does, why it's different than the old way people used computers and the Web, and why people are giving two hoots about it, here are some thoughts to start the conversation. I look at this mostly from a business perspective, but I suspect you'll find these apply to nonprofits and other organizations as well. Further, as I'm fond of saying, social media isn't relegated to the marketing and PR teams. It's a bunch of tools that can be used throughout businesses, in different forms.

Think about the things social media does best:

- Blogs allow chronological organization of thoughts, status, ideas. This means more permanence than e-mails.
- Podcasts (video and audio) encourage different types of learning—and in portable formats.
- Social networks encourage collaboration, can replace intranets and corporate directories, and can promote non-e-mail conversation channels.
- Social networks can amass like-minded people around shared interests with little external force, no organizational

center, and a group sense of what is important and what comes next.

- Social bookmarking means that entire groups can learn of new articles, tools, and other Web properties instead of leaving them all on one machine, one browser, for one human.
- Blogs and wikis encourage conversing, sharing, creating.
- Social software, like Flickr,[2] Last.fm,[3] and even Amazon .com, promote human-mediated information sharing. Similar mechanisms inside of larger organizations would be just as effective.
- Social news sites show the popularity of certain information, at least within certain demographics. Would roll-your-own voting within the company be useful?
- Social networks are full of prospecting and lead-generation information for sales and marketing.
- Social networks make for great ways to understand the mind-set of the online consumer, should that be of value to you.
- Online versions of your materials and media, especially in formats that let you share, mean that you're equipping others to run with your message, should that be important (e.g., if you're a marketer).

---

[2] www.Flickr.com
[3] www.Last.fm

- Online versions of your materials and media are searchable, and this helps Google to help you find new visitors, customers, and employees.
- Social networks contain lots of information about your prospective new hires, your customers, your competitors.
- Blogs allow you to speak your mind and let the rest of the world know your thought processes and mind-sets.
- Podcasts are a way to build intimacy with information.
- Podcasts reach people who are trying out new gadgets, like Droids, iPhones, iPods, Apple TVs, Zunes, and more.
- Tagging and sharing and all the other activities common on the social Web mean that information gets passed around much faster.
- Human aggregation and mediation improves the quality of data you find and gives you more "exactly what I was looking for" help. (See also Mahalo.[4])
- Innovation works much faster in a social software environment, open source or otherwise.
- Conversations spread around, adding metadata and further potential business value.
- People feel heard.

And that's a great place to ask you what I've missed. What else does social media do best, in your estimation?

---

[4]www.mahalo.com/

3

Social Media Does Not Replace Marketing Strategy

In yet another moment of informational threading, here's a post by Dan Kennedy[5] about hyperproductive markets. Kennedy points out that knowing your rough sales target is one thing, but knowing the most productive and yielding part of the whole bunch is worth so much more.

Thread this together with Robert Middleton's[6] post about a karate model for marketing. There's a lot to it, but the key point was something he took out of another presentation he'd seen, which was this:

1. *You first have to get your clients and customers to consume what you've already sold them.*
2. *You need to offer new services in progressively more complex stages if you are going to truly serve them.*

---

[5]http://dankennedy.com
[6]http://actionplan.blogs.com/weblog/2008/07/the-karate-model-of-marketing.html

I'm working on launching a few new things at work, and they are projects that have strong social media and new marketing elements to them. In so doing, I'm thinking a lot about what these tools can do for the communities we serve, and I'm also thinking about the marketplace elements that my business will need to sustain all this. My company is in the business of helping people connect, learn, and do business together. We do this through creating content, building online and face-to-face events, and enabling a marketplace between people selling emerging technologies and people looking to understand which of these technologies will help them next.

Kennedy's point about understanding that there's a group of people you can sell to, but within that group lies a more productive area, is useful. Middleton's point about having some kinds of selective level-ups[7] in your marketing efforts struck a chord insofar as one might consider narrowing the potential funnel for specific products and services (and thereby marketing efforts) once you move deeper into territory that applies to only a select few.

SOCIAL MEDIA LETS YOU GO WIDE, BUT *YOU* HAVE TO MAKE IT GO DEEP

The tools we use to create social media (blogging, podcasting, video, social networks, etc.) are great at building potential

---

[7] In games, leveling up is when you reach the end of a series of activities, face a big challenge, and then move to the next level. http://chrisbrogan.com/how-to-level-up/

relationships, growing community, serving an audience, helping people find your business, and several other things.

But social media tools alone are not especially built to carve out more productive customers on their own. That still requires a strategy that includes surrounding marketing and products to help convert potential segments of the community into potential business customers. And remember, as I'm fond of saying: Be clear about who makes up the community at large and who makes up your marketplace, because confusing the two can be deadly.

MY TAKEAWAYS AND YOUR IDEAS

From those two articles, I have taken away the following:

- Data and understanding who makes up your community is still crucial, no matter the toolset.
- Social media tools will be useful in communicating with the community members to understand their needs.
- Sorting out the early "grazers" from the committed buyers will help both sides of your community.
- Finding ways to help your audience "level up" within the community would help the whole process.
- I need to read even more outside of social media to bring it back home to how I use the tools.

Did you read the articles? What did you take from them? How are you working on this within your organization?

4

Making Business
Sense of Social Media

Quite simply, social media is a new set of communication and collaboration tools that enable many types of interactions that were previously not available to the common person. Blogging and video blogging and podcasting are lead-generation tools or content marketing. Twitter is part customer service, part marketing, part team collaboration (and overall, the new social phone's key component). These tools are a lot more than just shiny things the kids are using.

In defining how they all work in sales and marketing, realize that using listening tools means that salespeople can listen for new prospects, hear their opportunities and complaints, and learn what others are saying about your products and your competitors. In understanding how these tools empower a new form of gatejumping customer service, learn what Comcast and Dell and Rackspace and Home Depot and the Roger Smith Hotel and many other companies have learned: People are talking about you. You have to answer.

There are business opportunities everywhere for these tools. I'm working primarily with Fortune 100 companies on executing these, in community management, content marketing, presence management, or enhanced outreach. We develop sales channels with these tools. We supercharge event experiences to improve leads. We augment marketing materials and build community experiences around brands and products.

There's lots more to this. You and I will approach this from lots of angles. Stay with me.

5

Social Media as Personal Power

Enterprise software isn't very sexy. I agree with Robert Scoble's[8] perspective on this. And though others are disagreeing with this, people like Nick Carr[9] are seeing Scoble's point. The conversation around the argument is that enterprise applications aren't meant to be sexy; they're meant to work flawlessly for the organization. Well, here's where it's interesting to me.

---

[8]http://scobleizer.com/2007/12/09/why-enterprise-software-isnt-sexy/
[9]www.roughtype.com/archives/2007/12/michael_krigsma.php

SOCIAL MEDIA WORKS FOR YOU

Every tool that social media counts in its arsenal—blogging, podcasting, video blogging, microblogging (Twitter,[10] Posterous,[11] Tumblr[12]), and all the rest—is a tool equipped to offer you personal power. How do I mean this?

- *Social media gives you a voice.* Though some organizations have strict policies against blogging about that organization, it'd be hard for them to stop you from blogging about other areas of interest, your passions, and things that don't relate to your day job.
- *Social media gives you an audience.* Instead of waiting for mainstream media to determine whether your thoughts are worthy of a larger audience, you have the *chance* to build an audience from day one. (And believe me, there's someone for everyone out there.)
- *Social media gives you flexibility.* Are you better in pictures? Use Flickr. Not very tech savvy? Use Utterli. A budding Kubrick? Make a video blog. Hemingway? Write a blog.
- *Social media gives you a world audience.* Okay, what happens inside the firewall is one thing, but what happens out on the Internet goes pretty much everywhere (which is a caution as well as a benefit).

---

[10]www.Twitter.com
[11]http://Posterous.com
[12]www.Tumblr.com

WAYS TO ENHANCE SOCIAL MEDIA POWER

Should you wish to use your media for something beyond expressing yourself, there are many ways available for you to develop a following and to tap this audience for the better good of your community. Consider some of the following:

- Find like-minded media makers. If you're blogging about developing nations or nonprofits, find great people like Beth Kanter.[13] If you're writing about presentations, get connected to Heidi Miller[14] and Presentation Zen.[15] There's strength in numbers.
- Use Twitter to develop relationships by *communicating* with people and finding folks who are interested in the things that you find interesting.
- Contribute to others' projects, and be useful. Think of way upon way upon way to be useful.
- Help people connect. This is a gesture that people seldom forget. Those who continue to give of themselves find themselves with great friends and an active, engaged community.

The core of this idea is that there's strength in numbers. One voice is but a raindrop. Many voices is a flood. (This is an

---

[13]http://beth.typepad.com/

[14]http://heidimillerpresents.com/

[15]www.presentationzen.com/

echo of an audio ad made by Christopher S. Penn[16] for the first ever PodCamp, and it has forever stayed with me.)

USE YOUR POWER FOR GOOD

Social media can help you do many things, from simple things like finding a job (lots of us use our blogs as a sort of living resume) to participating in world-changing events and great social causes.[17] Of all the benefits of building a community of active voices, perhaps the greatest is that you can use this ability to help others.

DIFFERENT THAN AN ENTERPRISE APPLICATION

Social media tools are built to connect individual voices to a community. The basic unit of all (most?) social media applications is the individual. We can join groups in Facebook, but we start with an individual profile. We can follow people we like in Twitter and add friends in Seesmic,[18] but we are first and foremost a production company of one.

Further, social media tools do a great job of capturing unstructured information, as Rachel Happe from IDC pointed out in her speech on social networks in the enterprise. Use this difference for the power it's worth. Use things like blogs and

---

[16]www.christopherspenn.com/
[17]http://twitter.com/santacause
[18]http://Seesmic.com

Utterz[19] and wikis to gather and annotate and stretch and link and meta-organize information that doesn't have a home in more formal settings.

As an added bonus, social media tools can act perfectly as a crossover tool. For instance, you can use Twitter with colleagues *and* with friends from other organizations (depending on corporate policies, of course). You can blog for ideas, inspiration, and collaboration and use what you learn to develop your professional projects. These tools are perfect for the occasional task of shoring up your flagging interest in your day job, by showing you that engaged minds are out there doing amazing things.

WHERE'S YOUR CAPE?

We kicked off the first PodCamp[20] by saying that everyone in the audience was a superhero. They had their day jobs, their Clark Kent lives, but then they had these tools and this community that extended far beyond the firewall. People inside a PodCamp relate to each other in ways that don't mirror the typical corporate hierarchy.

At PodCamp Europe, we had people from Nokia and Ericsson in the audience, listening and responding to the sessions without competition. We frequently have Apple and Microsoft employees in the audience. It's easy to forget about

---

[19]www.Utterz.com

[20]http://PodCamp.org

the competitive, dog-eat-dog world when you're at a PodCamp because people there are more interested in learning the tools, developing community, and building a stronger relationship with communities of interest.

I grew up in Maine. I love it there, but there were plenty of times when I felt out of step with the folks living in my proximity. As the Internet developed, so did my opportunities to reach out and communicate with like-minded people. And now, with all these tools, I have the power to communicate and hold conversations in many ways with exceptionally diverse groups.

That's the power of all this. It's not Google juice. It's not a new way to market to people. It's sure not about re-creating media on the Net. Connections. Pure, quality connections. You need only read these two[21] recent posts by Shel Israel to see the power *you* wield.

Now, how will you use it? How *are* you using it? What do you think about this talk of empowerment and ability?

---

[21]http://redcouch.typepad.com/weblog/2007/12/lionel-at-dell.html

6

Social Media for Your Career

Today's career environment is different, at least for the information workers. What's different is that there are more ways to influence getting a job than in the past. You probably already know that this old saying is true: "It's not what you know; it's who you know." Well, the number of people you know has expanded a bit, thanks to social networks, and what people know about you has grown, too, thanks in part to the various tools you can employ in social media.

What follows are some ideas on building your online presence with your career in mind.

YOUR BLOG IS A RESUME

If you've not considered this yet, let me explain that my blog has been responsible for *hundreds* of inquiries over the years. Why? Because people who might want to know about using video or blogging or making podcasts or tying this all together into a strategy see examples, almost daily, of what I think, what I know, and how I've accomplished some of this in my own life and career.

Blogging about this stuff is like writing out my experience for a resume, line by line (only less boring).

Use These Tools for You

The story of our work lives, and the story of what we do after work when we're expressing our passion, can now be captured in ways we didn't have available to us before. With free tools and free or inexpensive distribution, you can share your accomplishments with the world, and with Google, which most prospective employers use as a matter of course these days in their hiring diligence.

ELEMENTS TO CONSIDER

Once you start thinking of your blog as a way for people to know more about you, what you stand for, and who you are, you might consider doing a few things.

- Consider placing your picture on the main page. I admit that I take this to extremes, but so be it. You won't ever *not* recognize me at a conference or a social event, and that's my goal.
- Make your "About" page robust. I write a lot about who I am, where to find me, what I am passionate about, and other things on my About page. In my case, I even have a speaking[22] page, so people know what I speak about at events (or some of what I speak about).
- Make it easy to contact you. My e-mail is right there on the blog, as well as my phone number. People use them both all the time, and these bring me interesting opportunities that don't always land in the comments section.

---

[22]www.chrisbrogan.com/connect/

- Consider *what* you talk about in your blog. Even if you don't consider your blog your resume, Google will help your prospective employers figure out your Web presence.

THE SOCIAL MEDIA RESUME

Listing your previous jobs and titles is not nearly a full picture of who you are, what you know, what you're capable of, and whom you know. There are other ways to do this. You might want to give some thought to posting more information about you online. There are ways to do this that don't seem so threatening to current employers, by the way.

If you haven't considered using LinkedIn,[23] that's a baseline. But LinkedIn is still a resume of sorts, with a few (really useful) features added in. LinkedIn can be explained to wary employers as a way to network with fellow professionals in your field and to find people who share interests. But don't stop there.

A few people have talked about a social media resume. My first exposure to it was Bryan Person's post[24] about it, with a link to his own social media resume. I've not employed this specifically, because I feel my profile on LinkedIn[25] covers all that ground, but I could see someone choosing to split their professional credentials from their social media experience, and then this would be the right tool.

---

[23]www.LinkedIn.com

[24]www.bryper.com/2007/10/08/die-resume-die-die-die/

[25]www.linkedin.com/in/chrisbrogan

SOCIAL NETWORKS FOR NETWORKING

First, I have to say that I have a problem with the notion of traditional networking, in the social sense. I perceive networking to mean those cocktail gatherings where you stand around and ask each other what you can do for each other. Though I understand it's usually genuine in intent, I've rarely found the right kind of relationship by doing the cursory dance at these events. Too shallow for my tastes.

Online social networks are different, insofar as we have the opportunity to know more about someone through repeated interactions. If you and I are friends on Twitter, I get to see what you deem interesting enough to post into a box. If we're friends on Facebook, I might learn a *lot* about your interests and the like from what you put on your profile, which groups you belong to, and your other posted media.

One more thing about Facebook[26]: The question of whether it's for business is coming from people who aren't in there messing around with it. It's not the best thing in the world for businesses, and I can tell you lots of things I hate about it, but it's a way to find a more enriched profile of someone than you get on LinkedIn, and that's the value statement there.

I think social networks, blogs, and all these various places like Twitter, Facebook, and Flickr, are great touchpoints to understanding someone's personal interests and tastes, and to learn about their professional proclivities as well.

---

[26]www.Facebook.com

THE BONUS ROUND

You might consider putting up a video about yourself. There's something different and more intimate about making video, and people can see more about who you are and how you act in a video.

One friend, Ben Yoskovitz, made a start-up out of the idea of video in recruiting.[27] It's brilliant, really, because it adds that piece that's missing.

And making video isn't especially hard these days. You can use a Flip video camera and pop a video onto YouTube without a lot of effort.

Now, making a *good* video is another matter altogether, but you might consider getting some help from a local expert.

A NOTE ABOUT *WHERE* TO FIND JOBS

This has changed a great deal over the past few years. Popular blogs and web sites now have their own job boards (e.g., 37 Signals,[28] TechCrunch,[29] and tons of other places). It's not just

---

[27] http://standoutjobs.com/site/
[28] http://37Signals.com
[29] www.TechCrunch.com

the world of Monster[30] or HotJobs.[31] Now, people and individuals are becoming hubs for jobs. Oh, and don't forget Craigslist.[32]

At any given time, I have someone pinging me for either a social media position that's open, or a software engineer, or someone with an Internet skill set that isn't easy to find by sifting through resumes. So be attentive to that as well. Sometimes, jobs aren't circulating in the traditional places, and the folks who might want to find you are the same ones spending time online.

7

Threading Some Trends Together

There's something afoot, and it deals with several pieces of economic pie shifting at the same time. In fact, it's a little strange that Richard Florida's latest book, *Who's Your City? How the Creative Economy Is Making Where to Live the Most Important Decision of Your Life,* is so timely. For a little more trend connection, throw

---

[30]www.Monster.com
[31]http://HotJobs.com
[32]www.Craigslist.org

in a little bit of Seth Godin[33] from May (this has stuck with me since then).

If you are an employer, think about the following.

CONNECTIVITY IS EVERYWHERE

It costs you more money to house a work staff than it does to manage them remotely. Consider items such as cost per cubicle, cost per in-house service, cost per enterprise service license, your network bandwidth costs, your power and cooling costs, all the things you have to do to keep people comfortable in an office space.

Afraid of how they'll work?

Shift measurements from "being there" to "what you've done." Look for deliverables that are based on pieces of information, goals met, business moved forward.

I'm on Verizon EVDO and writing this by the lake where I took my daughter swimming. I can work *anywhere* there's a signal. So can a lot of us. In fact, I do my job much better at a remote location (plus, it saves four hours of driving, two each way, at $66 a tank of gas twice or more a week).

THE LOOSELY JOINED EMPLOYEE

The age of half-owned brands is upon us. Years ago, it was only Robert Scoble. We watched in awe as he put a whole new face

---

[33]http://sethgodin.typepad.com/seths_blog/2008/05/the-new-standar.html

on Microsoft. He then shifted over to PodTech, and it didn't feel so strange. Was it strange at FastCompany? At Rackspace? Kind of. Look at the latest print issue of *FastCompany* and see how many times it mentions one employee, and not the boss.

Charlene Li leaving Forrester is actual news to a lot of us in this space. Why? Because probably five years ago, everyone would clamor to get *in* to Forrester. By the way, I think it's a great company, with good people, and all that. That's not my point.

Jeremiah Owyang left a little while later, to rejoin Charlene at Altimeter. Forrester's rock stars have mostly fled the coop, but it's not about Forrester. It's the trend. It's everywhere.

What about Chris Brogan as a brand? I went from employee with Jeff Pulver to employee with Stephen and Nick Saber to president of a company started with Stephen and Nick. In all of these moves, I maintained a mix of my own personal brand as well as support for the company that paid me. I think this will be a trend. As businesspeople, keep "deep benches" in mind.

HOW WHERE MATTERS

Seth Godin's post about conferences and workplaces[34] strikes home doubly for me. I'm in the conference business (at least, part of my money comes from events). It's my duty to convince thousands of people that I've got great speakers, engaging exhibitors, and passionate attendees for them to meet.

---

[34]http://sethgodin.typepad.com/seths_blog/2008/05/the-new-standar.html

Shel Israel's post[35] says that more businesses will use social media tools for economical reasons, for one:

> Businesses will increasingly use social media to get closer with customers. This, of course, is already happening and happening at a pretty fast rate. But I think the trend is about to accelerate. Because it is getting too expensive and inconvenient to meet face-to-face in the real world, there will be more efforts to bring the conversation to the next best place, in the form of virtual communities.

Steve Rubel says:

> Digital Nomads[36] are growing in numbers and they will create ripples. This trend will accelerate use of Web 2.0 technologies in the workplace. Over time, this may slow the efficacy of e-mail marketing and accelerate the reliance on social media engagement.

> However, it goes deeper than that. If you don't allow your employees to become nomadic, they may do so and even compete against you in the process.

WHERE WILL THIS GO?

In the very near term, I think a few things happen. I think that employers are definitely in a spot where they might have to

---

[35]http://redcouch.typepad.com/weblog/2008/07/social-media-th.html
[36]www.DigitalNomads.com

consider how their employees work. On one side, the management challenges are huge. It's not easy to shift around leadership and management styles. On the other hand, when there are cost savings to be had, a shift in flexibility might provide some hidden rewards. (Flex hours did this for a lot of companies. Suddenly, they had what amounted to shift workers without having to pay a premium.)

I also think that the idea of employees-as-brands-as-employees will stir more bees in the shorter term, but might start to make more sense as we become more comfortable with that lifestyle. Businesses are primarily organized in 1950s-era style right now. If we can adapt measurements and management style, I believe the downstream benefits are going to outweigh the interim headaches. Will all employees at all businesses feel these changes? No. And at least some employees will still have to be hands-on and nearby. (By the way, lots of people can't manage themselves very well and can't work remotely because they're easily distracted.)

One of our clients, Citrix Online, worked with us to launch the blog Workshifting.com, which talks specifically about this. We write together about the mobile and distributed workforce. This isn't a maybe. It's a now, and a "now what?"

Fuel costs are rising. Bandwidth is everywhere. Jobs are shifting into knowledge delivery and networked communities rather than face-to-face affairs.

It sure makes for a complex picture, but I don't know that we're going to stop it.

What do you say? Could you work remotely? Do you? How has the price of fuel affected you? What motivates you to attend a face-to-face event these days? Will you be changing your conference-going trends in the coming years? How about your hiring trends?

The Vital Importance of Your Network

Two great posts I found online show me that it's not just me thinking about this. Tim Sanders says we should refresh our network[37] often, and Jeremiah Owyang reports on the risks and opportunities[38] inherent in your network. It's all pointing toward the same thing: You have to think consciously about how you use social networks, and you have to build relationships that are decoupled from goals.

---

[37]http://sanderssays.typepad.com/sanders_says/2008/07/refresh-your-ne.html

[38]www.web-strategist.com/blog/2008/07/22/the-intangible-risk-and-opportunity-your-network/

KEEP YOUR NETWORK ALIVE

In his presentations, Christopher S. Penn frequently quotes a phrase I use that visionary community and event builder Jeff Pulver told me on the first day of work: "You live or die by your database." Remember that I do lots of events, and that's partially why I say that, but it's also true for people in all areas of business. Think about this:

If you lose your job today, how many people can you reach, and who would be helpful? Think harder about the names of those people. Have you talked with them lately in *any* form?

How do you stay connected to your network's news? Do you watch the news stream on LinkedIn? Do you watch the updates on Facebook, FriendFeed,[39] and other social networks? Spending 20 minutes or less on these platforms often gives you some interesting pieces of information, and might sometimes prompt a message out to people in your network.

Here are some practices to consider:

- Spend 20 minutes a day observing your network. If someone is mostly offline and not a social network user, spend a few minutes sending out a few "checking in" e-mails to get a read on his or her world.
- Spend 10 minutes a day (I spend a bit more here) cultivating new relationships. This can be through participation in social networks, through reading new blogs and commenting, through attending face-to-face events, or

---

[39]http://FriendFeed.com

many other things. If you're not growing your network, you're stagnating.

- Use an organized contact management system, but also keep frequent backup copies of those system's files in CSV or XLS form somewhere safe (i.e., don't trust online platforms 100 percent with your data). I'm using BatchBook[40] right now. (Disclosure: BatchBook gave me a complimentary license in return for a review, but it's still inexpensive, even if you pay.)

- Never, never, never pound that list of names with dumb jokes, updates about your life (unless it's something insanely profound), or other clutter. Try not to message *everyone,* ever. Instead, segment information such that you talk to the people who matter to the topic at hand.

- Deliver two to three times as much value as you ask from your network. This keeps people eager to be helpful when the time comes that you need them.

- Never make a huge deal out of helping others in your network.

- It's okay to say no (politely!) to requests for access through your network should you be concerned about the intent of the person asking.

TELL ME ABOUT YOUR NETWORK

How has your network impacted the way you live or conduct business? Do you belong to any networks, online or offline, that

---

[40]http://batchblue.com/

have driven value back to you? (My business partner is a Harvard Business School graduate, and the database he can touch is astounding.) How are you keeping your database fresh and vibrant?

Finally, are you living your online life consciously with regard to building and maintaining a meaningful network?

9

Using Social Networking and Media Offline

A great friend of mine mentioned that all my social media stuff was great but that he was frustrated because a lot of his constituency wasn't particularly connected to the Net and didn't really use computers too often. It came to me pretty quickly that computers really aren't a hard-and-fast requirement for attempting to get the same results I often preach about. In fact, it kind of opened my own eyes, too.

SOCIAL NETWORKING ONLINE TO OFFLINE

Online: Status message, as in Twitter or Facebook.
Offline: Quick phone call to see whether someone's going to be at an event.
Online: Blog post.

Offline: Letter or newsletter.
Online: Friending.
Offline: Meeting new people at networking events.

SOCIAL MEDIA ONLINE TO OFFLINE
Online: Flickr.
Offline: Mail some photos to people.
Online: Podcasts.
Offline: Mail them a CD.

YOU GET THE POINT

Essentially, you can do most of what you do online in the offline setting. It just takes a little longer and is a little less convenient. Yet the *motivation* behind what we do in the social networking space can be carried forth offline, and it would probably help us a bit to do so.

10

Velocity, Flexibility, Economy

Think that social media has nothing to offer your "traditional" business? I can give you reasons along any of three points of view: velocity, flexibility, and economy. As our tools come closer and closer to approximating and/or enhancing human interaction and further away from requiring an abundance of technological expertise, those who are exploring and sampling these tools are at an advantage that can be measured in speed, adaptability, and cost of operation.

We aren't talking about the marketing department. We aren't equipping PR professionals. This isn't a new set of tools for launching campaigns. These are tools to improve interaction, and they are incredibly powerful and game-changing ideas when you consider that most of these solutions have much less impact on traditional business resources.

VELOCITY

In the United States, in 2008, a "smart" cellular phone costs as little as $150 for the device and under $50 for an account with a data plan. Wifi hot spots are on the rise. A reasonably good laptop with built-in wireless capabilities can be purchased for under $500. With these two types of units as the base system, we can deliver the following capabilities:

- Instant communication in voice, text, e-mail, photo, video, and even geolocative
- Information browsing, including SMS-based and voice search (Google[41])
- Presence status information (Twitter, Jaiku,[42] Six Apart[43])

---

[41]www.Google.com

[42]www.Jaiku.com

[43]www.SixApart.com

- Shared documents (Google Docs[44])
- Voice conferencing (FreeConferenceCall[45] and tons more)
- Access to thousands of Web-stored applications and data

All without a cubicle. All without an office, an office manager, any infrastructure whatsoever. We can work out of coffee shops and libraries, at hotels and in the upstairs office, on the side of the road, or across the globe. Fast.

FLEXIBILITY

As recently as five years ago, we considered which software our organizations would buy based on the operating systems we supported. (Maybe yours still does.) Before that, we had to choose between token ring and Ethernet, beta and VHS. (Now there's Blu-ray and HD DVD, but you're not falling for that, right?) Today, we are flexible. There are some considerations to be had, but with *so many* applications running in the cloud, accessible through browsers, so much of what we choose to equip ourselves with is a personal choice, and it is a matter of our Internet access more than any other deciding factor.

- Office apps via Google or Zoho,[46] or desk versions from OpenOffice

---

[44]http://docs.google.com
[45]www.FreeConferenceCall.com
[46]www.Zoho.com

- Operating systems for free with Ubuntu (and hundreds of other Linux distributions), are irrelevant with the browser being our true compatibility choice
- Collaboration through wikis, shared spaces like Facebook, or in Ning[47] communities
- Conversations across multiple instant messaging (IM) vendors via Adium,[48] Trillium,[49] or Meebo[50]
- Blog on WordPress,[51] Blogger,[52] Movable Type,[53] Vox,[54] whatever
- Instant databases through Freebase[55] or Zoho
- File storage through Box[56] and so many more
- Video hosting from Blip.tv,[57] Brightcove,[58] YouTube[59]

We can choose from any number of sources, mix and match. Flexibility is abundant. You don't have to choose what your neighbor chooses. E-mail can be Gmail, Yahoo!, and whatever else.

---

[47]www.Ning.com

[48]http://Adium.im

[49]www.Trillium.im

[50]www.Meebo.com

[51]http://WordPress.com

[52]www.Blogger.com

[53]www.Movable Type.com

[54]www.Vox.com

[55]www.Freebase.com

[56]http://Box.net

[57]www.Blip.tv

[58]www.Brightcove.com

[59]www.YouTube.com

Just use a domain forwarding/POP3 scheme to maintain consistency with external sources.

ECONOMY

Why pay for it when you can use it for free? Cost doesn't imply reliability any more than free predicts uptime. Google is free and it is more diverse than any of your data centers. If you have to consider budget when considering social media, as with the rest of the premise, things fall back to the humans involved. Lots of companies are using ad-supported software models. Others are using services and add-ons and behind-the-firewall implementations to support their efforts. The point is still the same: You don't have to pay anything (or much) to get into the game.

- Use Skype[60] for free voice conversations (and cheap for SkypeOut).
- Use WordPress.com for free blog hosting, or Blogger, or Vox, or Tumblr.
- Facebook is free. Twitter is free. Gmail is free. Google Docs are free.
- Wikis are free. Freebase is free. Zoho is free.
- *Storage* is cheap (not free) for people making media. Price out 500 gigabytes of storage these days and you'll see that it costs less than you used to pay for a box of floppies in the mid-1990s.

---

[60]www.Skype.com

There are other costs in retooling your business practices and the like. Yet what's the return? If you're faster, more flexible, and have cost the company nothing in licensing, what have you hurt?

Beware of those selling you "solutions" that are "more robust" than what's out there for free. What's out there is working just fine for lots of people. People out beating the street doing important things are using these free apps, these Web-minded apps, these "you can't always be connected to the Internet" apps.

What's holding you back? What are the reasons you're hearing for *not* using social computing technology to enhance the way people do business at your company?

11

Snake Oil in Social Media

Justin Kownacki, creator and producer of the hit Web sitcom, *Something to Be Desired*,[61] friend, PodCamp Pittsburgh

---

[61]www.somethingtobedesired.com/

organizer, and many other things, had a great post[62] questioning what qualifies someone to be a social media expert. Quite rightly, he questioned me about my application of the term *expert* to my experiences and understanding of the space. In this community, it's important to question, to be critical, and to keep our motives and our expression of these things clear and transparent. This led me to consider the label of "expert" and to parse what it might mean to people seeking information in the social media space.

EXPERT OR ADVISER

Hours after reading that post by Justin, I was rereading a part of David Maister's *Strategy and the Fat Smoker,* an excellent book on how to get people to do the things they know they should be doing. Maister points out that labeling oneself an *expert* is sending the signal that the expert is in control, that he or she is to be heeded above others, and that the client needs the expert to complete the transaction.

Maister goes on to say that an *adviser,* on the other hand, is someone in a relationship with the client, someone who wants to offer opinions based on his or her experience, while adding into the mix a level of give-and-take and conversation. An expert, in Maister's parlance, is someone seeking a one-night stand, whereas an adviser is someone looking for romance. (I highly

---

[62]http://justinkownacki.blogspot.com/2007/12/what-makes-social-media-expert.html

recommend *Strategy and the Fat Smoker* for anyone interested in leadership and/or service relationships.)

I knew at once that I would change my branding on the sidebar of my web site to say "adviser." My reason is that I agree with Maister's assessment. I believe my interest is in having a relationship with an organization or an individual, one in which we talk about opinions and experience and where I help with potential outcomes. I agree because I am already an adviser to a handful of companies.

SOCIAL MEDIA AS A BUZZWORD

Every bit as overused as *Web 2.0,* the term *social media* is bandied about all the time. I define social media as "the two-way Web." This includes everything from blogging to video to podcasting to photo sharing and the use of social networks like Twitter and Facebook, for instance. The buzzword has slightly different meanings to different folks.

Some larger media companies make the term synonymous with "user-generated content," which they further view as amateurish, free, and in many ways inferior to "professionally generated content." I don't equate social media with user-generated content. (Further, I don't use the term *user-generated content* much, as I find that it's often used as a derogatory term.)

Is there a common ground to the term? I think it's one of those areas where we're all still feeling our way through the experience, and therefore we must be ready to question those who are discussing their knowledge of social media.

METRICS AND FAIRY TALES

One place where social media is still on shaky ground is in the application of metrics to various aspects of what we're doing. Podcasters, marketers, PR types, and others struggle with this all the time. Sponsors, clients, and customers of all types want to understand what they're buying.

Podcasters can't accurately report numbers that have concrete meanings. Do we count downloads? Do we count hits on a web page? Do we accept and adjust for the caching of our media such that we can't completely count or aggregate the impact of media we've made? Or do we find ways to make the action/response of the media felt? Christopher S. Penn doesn't exactly care how many people listen to the Financial Aid Podcast.[63] He cares how many people sign up for (and ultimately secure) a student loan, driven by his podcast. That's the purpose of his show: to educate, to inform, to build a level of trust and leadership, but ultimately, to drive people to purchase a loan through his organization. More metrics like this are needed for podcasters and video bloggers.

Empirical data is often the coin of the realm in business conversations. People rightly think that they want to understand the impact of their choices, the return on their investment. They feel comfortable that they understand how traditional marketing campaigns are measured. They believe they understand advertising purchases. When we shift into social media and social

---

[63] www.financialaidpodcast.com/

networks, even as online spending revenue is going up, we are faced with having to talk about the uncertainties and unknowns of how we measure impact.

Be ready to probe when people offer you empirical measurements of results. There are ways to derive what Julien Smith and others have called "return on influence," and there are means by which people are seeking to understand "cost-per-action-based pricing" instead of the more traditional online model of "cost per click." Be wary of what you hear in this space.

WHO ARE THE EXPERTS?

Let's press "pause" on the use of the word *expert* and instead consider who understands social media in a way that you might learn from their experience or seek their advice and recommendations. Here are a few things to look for in a good social media practitioner—and some things to discount:

- We don't know every social network that was ever built or every podcast currently or formerly in production, but we'd better know more than a few.
- Social media types probably should be making media of some kind themselves. (I am often criticized for not having a podcast. I counter by saying that I make media like Attention Upgrade,[64] Small Boxes,[65] and other projects.) And I blog every day and then some.

---

[64]http://attentionupgrade.magnify.net/
[65]http://smallboxes.blip.tv/

- We probably should have some length of experience under our belt, in some form or another. I've been blogging since 1998 or so, when it was called *journaling*. Long before that, I was into online places like AOL and bulletin board services. I'm newer to podcasting and video blogging (and I have Justin Kownacki and Steve Garfield to thank, two strong influencers and guiding lights in that space, not to mention folks like Daniel Steinberg and others, but don't let me digress here).

- We should be relatively "known." I'm not suggesting that popularity, in and of itself is important, but I do believe that if you're in *social* media and not many people know you yet, you might want to socialize some more. (This point is *very* open to your criticism, so please dig in if you disagree.)

- We should be able to make *something* happen by way of the media we create; in other words, our efforts should be at least somewhat impactful. I believe PodCamp has had an impact and that other things I've done have made little differences here and there.

- We shouldn't be afraid of transparency, and we definitely should welcome criticism and debate. If we're always right, we're probably not very open to ideas and new things. And at this point in the game, social media is heavily invested in understanding all kinds of new technologies and their applications.

Beyond that, what would *you* say qualifies someone to be spouting off about social media? Why do you bother coming to my site? What is your bar for accepting someone as an authority in this space? And do you need to learn *only* from a so-called authority, when plenty of people are experimenting and discovering advances every day? Beware the snake oil experts in any new technology, and question authority. It's worked as a good test since the 1960s. Why stop now?

12
Who Cares?

As a guy who does technology but has somehow found himself in a marketing-heavy role, I have a lot of opinions. Some might be wrong. You're always welcome to correct me if you disagree.

Marketers: Please, please, please think really hard about the recipient of your message. It seems *so* easy, but I find that people talk about how amazing they (their company, product, etc.) are. I'm glad you're proud, but is that what you want to tell me? Because if I'm the customer, consumer, user, and/or partner, do you know what I'm thinking, right?

- What's in it for me?
- How does this impact me?
- Do I have to do something?
- What's this going to cost me?

The other thing is this: Please rethink which details you think I might care about. I passed an ice cream truck the other day on the road. The side of it read: "Serving fresh ice cream since 1934." First, your ice cream *better* be fresh. Second, I don't care when you started. I want ice cream. Finally, ice cream is fun. People *love* ice cream. Why not talk about the fun?

Please, ask yourself after every little scrap of copy you write, "Who cares?"

13

Participation: The Key to Social Media

Creativity, creation, communities of interest, and culture itself are at the heart of what social media is equipped to enable. We view this area as a system of technologies, but even further down the stack, so to speak, is the simple realization that we have rediscovered our inherent right to be creative and to participate in the creative experience.

Somewhere in the early 1900s in America, creative culture shifted from being strongly participatory (people got together to sing songs, reading off their most recent subscription of sheet music) to being a consumer experience (people gathered around the radio to hear bands perform). This gave rise to new opportunities for more people to hear better performers, but it also shifted our attention away from the two-way experience of people creating their own culture (at least in part).

Larry Lessig delivered an important talk[66] about creativity and the law at the March 2007 TED Talks[67] event. He highlighted how the advent of broadcasting technology led to the creation of ASCAP, which sold music licenses to radio networks. Between 1931 and 1938, ASCAP raised licensing fees to broadcasters 448 percent. These concepts, these constructs, were set in place more than 70 years ago, and in that time, legal protection and safeguarding of the *business* of creativity has ratcheted up again and again, until copyright in America is a broken experience, to say the least.

READ-WRITE CULTURE

Lessig goes on to show some creative examples of the mashup culture in action, where talented people create new works derived from existing media. Hip-hop showed how sampling other artists' tracks could lead to derivative work that was unique in its new presentation, while building on cores of memory and shared awareness of other work.

What's changed in recent years is that technology is much more readily available, simpler to use, and media is far more

---

[66]www.ted.com/talks/view/id/187

[67]www.ted.com

widely distributed. This means that you and I have the building blocks to make something new, something creative, something fun using parts of others' works, as well as adding something new to the experience.

ABOUT CREATIVE COMMONS

If you are not yet familiar with the work of Creative Commons,[68] please spend some time on this site. Learn about the work of Lessig, Colette Vogel, and many other talented individuals working to open up new structures for participation and collaboration. Creative Commons is a legal licensing structure that enables creative works to be used in much more flexible ways than does a traditional copyright. Should you be interested in participating in social media, please consider applying Creative Commons licensing to your work in place of standard copyright protection.

IN A CULTURE OF PARTICIPATION

The media we create, our blogs, podcasts, photos, art, and music, are creative works unto themselves, but as we consider social media, we might think about how we can work well with others. Somehow, as I'm writing this, it seems dry and legal, or business-y. But that's not my goal. Instead, I'm saying that creative culture is empowered by social media and Creative

---

[68]http://creativecommons.org/

Commons such that we can be much more playful and have more fun with our media.

I've seen countless Flickr projects where people post an interesting photo or set of photos, and then others form groups and projects around the original works, sometimes replicating, sometimes building on a theme, and other times deriving new works through collage and other mash-up methods. That's built right into the platform of Flickr; it's not an accidental experience.

IF YOU MAKE SOFTWARE

If you make software for a living, consider the fact that Flickr has built participation into the core functionality of its product. And it's showing up in places that you might expect would not normally offer such things.

Mint[69] is a personal finance Web application that uses some interesting sharing methods to model a group's general spending and investing habits. Users are anonymous in that regard (e.g., when sharing their investment choices), but because of the sharing function, people are able to better understand personal finance by observing the behavior of other users.

Sites like YouTube are "sticky" because people can comment in video and text form. They can subscribe, rate, share, and discover works on the site.

---

[69]www.mint.com/

Here are some more thoughts for software makers:

- Use and release APIs. Make your site as compatible with other media sites as possible.
- Make data portable, or at least some part of the data.
- Consider using the OpenID standard for login information.
- Realize that we, the users, are using tons of sites and applications, so don't make it too tricky or involved for us to use your site, too.

IF YOU MAKE MEDIA

Newspapers and other media sources are learning to integrate "citizen journalism" into their traditional hierarchical structures. Quality reporting doesn't always come from within, as evidenced by great projects such as Alive in Baghdad.[70] In this new world, people (or we might say "enabled and equipped people") are the important pieces of the puzzle. Larger news organizations need to learn how to integrate with a project like Brian Conley's Alive in Baghdad such that the news generated by average people on the streets in Iraq is mixed into the "professional" journalistic product, with little or no distinction between sources.

Think about that for a moment. If you are a media company, it is no longer good enough to make a little playground for your "fans" to "have their say." *We* are media makers now.

---

[70]http://aliveinbaghdad.org/

We are the media, too. And as such, it is no longer acceptable to enable commenting. Nice start, but you have to learn how to build your business with us in mind these days.

Media makers aren't always trained journalists. I'm definitely not. But we can contribute to the larger story, work with editors and curators (you'll learn that "curation" and "editing" become two very important skills on the social media landscape), and feel more connected to the ultimate work generated by this in the long run.

Here are some quick tips for media organizations:

- Treat independent producers like professionals.
- Empower two-way promotion of creative pieces, instead of just having a "fan area."
- Consider ways to modularize and/or use Creative Commons license for portions of your work.
- Seek ways to engage independent producers.

IF YOU ARE AN INDEPENDENT PRODUCER

I spent a good part of 2007 meeting with independent audio and video producers, talented and driven people with excellent shows and content. Some were re-creating television for this new age. Others pushed formats out entirely and simply lived life online. Still others used the various outlets to have conversations using social media tools. In all cases, these people were empowered (and felt empowered) simply because they had the tools and the opportunity to produce and release works of their own creation.

Some of the best of these producers made participation a cornerstone of their shows from the beginning. They worked to incorporate other creators. They empowered their audience base to be a core functionality of the show. They enabled their audience to share their show, helped to point out other producers' works that might complement what they were doing, and did a lot to raise up their interactions with their audience as a wholly participatory experience.

WAYS TO FOSTER PARTICIPATION

If you want to build strong participation into your social media projects, try to incorporate some of the following into your repertoire:

- License your content under an appropriate Creative Commons license. Make sure you are explicit about how you want to see your work used or shared by others.
- Enable (and participate in) commenting for your media.
- Consider building your content in modular fashion, or in ways it can be integrated, mashed up, or remixed. (Bands like the Barenaked Ladies have taken to releasing their digital masters to others to mix. Is there an analogous experience you can offer your audience?)
- Look for software and platforms that promote sharing, such as using Blip.tv to host your video-blogging projects.
- Support organizations and media makers who promote sharing and participation.

- Engage your audience such that they'd want to participate. Hold contests. Ask for their opinions and incorporate some of them from time to time.
- Turn the spotlight on your audience and point the micro-
  phone at them as often as you can. Make sure they know
  how valuable they are to you.
- Seems weird to put here, but be honest and trustworthy.
  It's pretty easy to break trust with your audience, and it's
  really difficult to win it back.

Participation is a core element of social media. It's a strong
portion of the "social" in social media. You probably have ways
of participating that I haven't listed here. What are they? What
else can we do to empower participation? Let's have a discussion
in the comment section at http://chrisbrogan.com/comments-
from-101.

14

Social Media Is a Set, Not a Part

Corporations are built of very distinct pieces. People understand
their jobs, their duties, and how they will be measured. This
very thinking is industrial in nature. It fits well in 1900s-era

thinking. If you are a machinist, your job is to turn out perfect gears. If you are a painter, your job is to paint your parts expertly and waste less paint. But in an age where pretty much everything about humanity is a mash-up (we do "work" in cafés; we build businesses by giving away products for free; we let our customers decide our designs), thinking of our organizations as specific pieces, or separate parts, might be the death of companies in the next few years.

A COMPLEX INTERACTION WITH SPILLOVER

My thoughts keep coming back to Rachel Happe from the Community Roundtable, who said that the main benefit and value of social networks (and social media, by extension) is to capture unstructured information that otherwise rushes past without a "bucket" to connect it to the "memory" of an organization. Meaning this: Lots of useful information that comes from making social media and using social networks benefits more than just one "department" at a business.

Let's illustrate this with an example:

- Ravi posts on his blog that he just bought the Garglesoft Bookreader, and it's not really all that great for what he wants it to do. He's mad that it won't let him download books from other sites that aren't Garglesoft.
- Natasha in Garglesoft customer relations sees this post in her "listening" RSS feed, and bookmarks it with

Del.icio.us,[71] such that her colleagues in other departments will get the post in *their* listening feeds.

- Sonya in Garglesoft engineering sees what Ravi has posted and realizes that it's not that the Bookreader *can't* do it, but that the feature just isn't as obvious as it seemed to internal engineers. Sonya Clipmarks[72] the part of Ravi's post she wants to highlight, drops it into an internal wiki, and then notates for the next release of the app how this might work differently. She tweets (or whatever the enterprise version of Twitter will eventually be) this update to her product management colleagues.

- Sonya then blogs on the Garglesoft Bookreader project blog (an external blog) showing Ravi's post and/or posts a screencast step-by-step explanation on how to do what Ravi wants to do. She concludes with a promise to review the feature for the next release of the Garglesoft Bookreader.

- Meanwhile, Ramesh in HR notes that Ravi has lots of great ideas in his previous blog posts, and he passes on Ravi's LinkedIn profile to the software engineering team, to consider Ravi for a future project.

In this example, customer relations, engineering, and HR departments all used social networks and social media. We could have layered in marketing (perhaps pointing to a collection of helpful how-to video-blog posts, etc.) and some

---

[71]http://delicious.com/

[72]http://clipmarks.com/

other departments, but you get the point, right? More than one department uses these tools in concert.

IS IT WORTH IT?

Taking this kind of approach with social networks and social media will eat into the time spent working on products. That's a reasonable opinion. I can see senior leadership worrying about that, and they'd be right if their people were not actually interacting with people with an interest in their products and services.

But what better way to stay plugged into the world of your customers than to try and be where they are?

Oh, and this raises another whole point. What if your business is B2B? What if your business is totally offline? What if your business has nothing in common with the Internet's demographics.

There are still ways to participate with social media. For instance, there are some great B2B blogs out there. There are some great podcasts that give you information on how people approach things in the offline world. You've got to look for them, but they're out there. Besides, if you're reading *Social Media 101,* it's pretty likely that your customer base is online, or that you've already figured out how to approach the offline world with what you learn here.

PLAYING THE CHESSBOARD, NOT THE PIECE

Learning to play chess means understanding how all the pieces work in concert. It means understanding how other players might focus on one piece, but neglect others. It means under-standing that things set up early in the game might execute later for a fuller impact. The same is true with implementing social media practices at an enterprise.

Look at your organization's informational needs. Don't start by pushing social media tools down people's throats, but instead look for the problems different parts of the organization might need to solve. In my Garglesoft example, I had Ramesh in human resources scanning blogs for potential suitable employees. Can you imagine your organization finding talented people by the media they make online? I know folks who have picked up their job from what they've put on their blog. (Um, me, for instance.)

How does your organization pass information around inter-nally with regard to projects? Could you see your organization's members benefiting from reading external sources of informa-tion? Do you know which tools would work best for them to aggregate all they've learned?

USE SIMPLE PIECES

Would your organization benefit from making media? Why not start with simple tools like Utterli, which works on any cell phone, and video tools like Magnify[73] or 12seconds.tv,[74] which let you record video straight from your browser using Flash[75]? As with learning chess, organizations probably should

---

[73]www.Magnify.net

[74]http://12seconds.tv/

[75]www.Adobe.com

learn simpler tools before moving into something more complex. (Although, as a side note, thinking about training and then retraining might make organizations consider their toolset more carefully before rolling out something half-baked to the world.)

HOW WOULD *YOUR* CORPORATION INTEGRATE SOCIAL MEDIA?

Could you see your company building social media and social networking tools into its practices? What would the barriers be? Where would your company stumble? Have you tried? What were the results? What was the push back?

15

Media Is a Mix— Get Mixing

Check out www.iEllie.com, a personal blog by a college student majoring in mass communications, which focuses on PR. Her blog is an interesting peek into the heads of college students and how they're viewing blogs, media making, and media consumption. Encapsulated on the first page alone are some interesting points to consider. And before you go and dismiss the blog for being unprofessional, or scattered, or anything else derisive, think creatively for a moment. Look at it as a mixing board, a paint palette. See what iEllie is putting out there; and from there, we can extrapolate.

IN THIS FIRST CAPTURE

Notice how iEllie uses a sideways picture in the banner. Fun, not pro. Fun. It shows a human, someone communicating. Then look: iEllie goes right into making media, with an Utterli post embedded at the top, a podcast right below. She shows all her related networks (tons!) and some personal data right on the front page; iEllie is out there, telling us who she is, but not giving away 100 percent of what a stalker would need (important point to consider).

MEDIA AND MOTION AND MEDIA SOME MORE

Packed into iEllie are pictures and podcasts and Flickr and tons and tons of production. She's creating all the time, and using the various formats interchangeably. This gives you a sense of the mix culture. It's not a blog. It's not a podcast. She's making something, and it doesn't *need* a name because there's a payload.

Key to the game: Forget the labels; focus on the payload.

WHERE IT GETS EVEN MORE COOL

In addition, iEllie posts YouTube clips right up there alongside her media. She doesn't single out one over the other. In fact, I'm going to bet that she doesn't distinguish between what she makes and what she finds, cultivates, and curates. Why should she? It's the same as clipping the words out of a magazine and forming your own sentence or writing on a page. It's the same output at the end.

WHY ALL THE FUSS OVER IELLIE.COM?

It's not about iEllie, specifically. I'm sure she's wonderful and all that. I just followed her on Twitter. But I see it as a way to illustrate simply all the various facets of media making, media usage, and media consumption in the coming year. If you want to distill it out, here's what I'm thinking should happen:

- Big media (journalistic, entertainment, etc.): You should divert *some* of the ad budget (0.01 percent?) to media-sharing projects, such as giving people mash-up clips of movies and songs.
- Marketers and advertisers: Have people *willingly* sharing stuff all over the place. Give your projects handles, and see if people will take them.
- PR types: Don't go after just the A-list bloggers. Find the iEllie's of the world, find legions of them, and get them into your campaign.
- Professionals and leaders of the world: iEllie is your next employee. Look at how she rolls. Is your business ready for her? It better be, because that's your job pool right there. Someone who mixes, mashes, uses *all* the social networks, someone who considers this the same as doing work for you.

- Parents: Are you equipping your kids to make media? (Don't get into a privilege story here.) If not, your kid is disadvantaged in this regard. Computers and the Internet and powerful tools aren't frivolous. Ditto game systems. Ditto *networked* game systems. *This* is our golf, people. Halo 3 and Tweetups are the new golf courses and country clubs. At least for some.
- Media makers: Are you purists? Are you mashing and reusing and mixing? Are you making it easier for people to share and use *your* media?

16

Social Media Starter Pack

Work of any kind requires an understanding of the appropriate tools for the job, and social media is no different. You can't pitch hay with a shovel, and you can't dig a ditch with a pitchfork. Here are some serving suggestions for a set of social media tools. The actual applications will change over time, because technology does that. But the basic functions should evolve a little more slowly.

LISTENING

In social media, as in life, listening is twice as important as speaking. Online, the tool for listening is a newsreader. This type of software allows you to understand the conversation going on out there, and the best newsreaders permit you to understand a little better what you're "hearing."

If you Google the phrase "grow bigger ears," you'll find a really quick way to start listening for free using some of the tools that I'm about to mention. (This gets a bit techy. If you feel twitchy about it, just skip this part for later. Throw in a bookmark or sticky note, or highlight it, and come back. It's okay.)

I recommend Google Reader. It's easy to use, has ways to roll through information quickly, supports the import and export of OPML (which is simply the bundle of all the feeds you've selected to follow), and has some powerful sharing features that make it more compelling to me than other readers.

What should you listen to? It depends on how you're intending to use the tool, but if you're part of a company in a certain space, here's a way to think of it:

- Build an ego search. Use tools like Technorati and Google Blogsearch to build a search on your company's name, your products' names, key employees' names, and so forth.
- Build the same for your competitors.
- Find blogs about your specific space or industry and subscribe to a handful of them. (It's easier to add tons and

subtract a few than to think you're getting the best and be missing something better.)

- Find a few tangential categories. If you're in software, subscribe to an art or marketing blog. If you're in marketing and PR, subscribe to an economy blog.
- Add in a few hobbies. This should help you use this reader more frequently. (Don't overdo it.)

There are several advanced listening tools that take the data you receive and help you make better sense of it. As of this writing, I'm partial to Radian6, because it's flexible and allows people to do a somewhat deeper dive on the information we gather. There are many tools in the advanced category, but I'll save that for some other time. At the time I'm writing this book, there are well over a dozen other professional listening tools in the space, each with their own angle on the world.

SPEAKING

Blogs and podcasts and video blogs and Twitter and dozens and dozens of other tools exist for speaking. It's almost too much to tell you about all the various platforms, because I could deliver hundreds and hundreds of things for you to check out. Most of you probably already use something that you're comfortable with and that you prefer. Instead, let's just talk about some ways to "improve" the quality of your speaking; in other words, here are some ideas about how your voice can be heard further.

- Use FeedBurner[76] to improve your RSS feed. No built-in RSS feed provides as many features and enhancements as FeedBurner. Bring your existing blog feed to Feed-Burner, make a new feed there, do all the little tweaks and add-ons suggested, and then promote *that* feed as your subscription mechanism to your media, no matter what form your media takes.

- Use Facebook and other social networks to point people toward your primary media. Use these services to tap into audiences that might not find your work otherwise. Seek out like-minded people who are making similar media, and share attention with them (meaning give them attention and offer your media as something they might like as well).

- Make sure your e-mail signature and your business card have your URL to your media. This is about reaching the people with your conversation.

- Make sure your site and all your media points back to you, so folks know who you are, where you are, how to reach you, and what you are all about.

COMMUNITY

Social networks abound. By the time this book is published, there will probably be another dozen launched. A week from now, there will be yet another 100 that aren't covered here.

---

[76]http://FeedBurner.com

Following are some thoughts about social networks, how you might use them for your social media experience, and a few that I like.

- *Twitter*. Twitter is simple and yet complex. You get 140 characters to say what you're doing or, if you use it a little differently, to tell people what has your attention. Twitter is a great place to meet people, to build digital relationships, and to add value to conversations. It's my current favorite social network.

- *Facebook*. The benefit of Facebook is that it's a place with millions of active users, and it has had a powerful growth curve in the past several months. If you don't already have a huge audience, Facebook is a good place to find people who might like what you're doing. It's also gaining ground as a place businesses are investigating.

- *LinkedIn*. It's a place for building an equivalent to your resume or curriculum vitae (CV), and that means it's another place to encourage people to interact with your media. List one of your current jobs as "publisher of a blog" or "media maker," and show people how to find your media there as well.

- *MySpace*[77] is appropriate if you have a youth element to your project or if you're in the music or entertainment space; this is not to be scoffed at, given that the user base of MySpace still far and away dwarfs other services.

---

[77]www.myspace.com

I have an out-of-date account there, and I should probably listen to my own advice and tidy it up.

- *Ning.* Ning is a great white-label social network opportunity, such that you can create a place for your audience if you already have a decent audience. It's very
  modular, offers RSS for all the various pieces, integrates
  well with third-party applications, and can be branded
  nicely with your existing properties. Several large media
  companies are using Ning now.

- *Other social networks.* There are *many* other networks with
  great pocket communities for various interests. I love
  how Flickr has built a community around photo sharing.
  Digg has built a strong community around tech news.
  There are all kinds of other examples. You will know.

RICH MEDIA

For content creation beyond blogging, I touch briefly on some
applications that I use to create media. There are *tons* of things
that make this tricky to just touch on. PC versus Mac. Price
point. Your ultimate goal. Here's a good starter pack for making audio and video podcasts for both PC and Mac.

- *Audio.* In both cases, I recommend Audacity[78]. It's free,
  open source, and works on several platforms. For Macs,
  GarageBand[79] is good, too. I haven't found the analog on

---

[78]http://audacity.sourceforge.net
[79]www.GarageBand.com

PC (you can tell me in comments at http://chrisbrogan .com/comments-from-101.) Other solutions without hardware could be Utterli and BlogTalkRadio,[80] each of which has its advantages and opportunities.

- *Video.* I use plain old iMovie, which comes with a Mac. You can use Windows Movie Maker on a PC with similar levels of skill. Beyond that, most folks swear by Final Cut Pro. I recommend Final Cut Express unless you're an amazing filmmaker and really want to make a new classic.

- *Video hosting.* There are many more choices here, each with advantages and challenges that I won't talk about in this book. You already know about YouTube, but really read the terms of service to understand whether that's a good choice for you. I strongly recommend Blip.tv, and beyond that, there are tons of great services, such as Vimeo,[81] Viddler,[82] Revver,[83] and more.

- *Live video.* Another new player in the works is live video.[84] You can create interesting and compelling opportunities with live video. Services such as Ustream,[85] BlogTV,[86] and Paltalk[87] offer different experiences in this world.

---

[80]www.BlogTalkRadio.com

[81]www.Vimeo.com

[82]www.Viddler.com

[83]www.Revver.com

[84]www.livevideo.com

[85]www.Ustream.tv

[86]www.BlogTV.com

[87]www.Paltalk.com

Beyond these four segments, I have a few more tools I'd like to recommend, in case you're not aware, or in case you have other suggestions for me.

- Firefox is my browser of choice. I like the power that the various add-ons bring to my Web browsing experience. Other people swear by Flock[88] as the social media browser of choice. You could try both and decide.
- Miro[89] is a free, open-source Internet TV and video player. It has some really great features, and allows you to discover great video content.
- Del.icio.us[90] social bookmarking has two benefits over using your browser's bookmark system: (1) You can get to it anywhere you have the Internet, and (2) you can discover new things from friends.
- Meebo[91] is a Web-based IM aggregator application that allows you to be logged in to various instant messaging clients. App versions include Adium and Trillian (Mac or PC, respectively).

You no doubt have some ideas on other stuff to add to the starter kit. So, what do you think? What have I missed? What do you disagree with here?

---

[88]www.Flock.com

[89]www.Miro.com

[90]http://delicious.com/

[91]www.Meebo.com

17

Five Starter Moves for Introducing Social Media into Your Organization

Companies are being pressured into the whole social media thing from lots of angles. They're reading about it in mainstream press more often. Their PR agencies are asking them about it. PR agencies themselves are being pressured into getting into social media and social networking. But what does it mean? Where should one start?

SEPARATE SOFTWARE FROM MOTIVATIONS AND PROCESS

First, mentally break the chain between social media and social networking being specifically about the software. If I were introducing elements of social media into an organization, and I do this very shortly, I'd start by explaining *why* one bothers to do this in the first place, *who* one might reach in the space, and *how* one might use these tools to listen better, have two-way dialogues, and collaborate creatively.

One way to help organizations understand is through case studies. Superstar authors Geoff Livingston and Brian Solis provided an entire section[92] of case studies to accompany their excellent *Now Is Gone*, a primer on new media for executives. It's a quick read, and inexpensive enough that you can buy a copy without expensing it.

In fact, pick up a copy to share with your team.

18

Five Starter Moves: Should Blogging Go Next?

In our Five Starter Moves[93] discussion so far, we've talked about framing the idea to our organization and about listening/hearing. Now, let's talk about blogging.

I ask this question because I believe most people advising organizations about social media go straight for a blog as their

---

[92]http://nowisgone.com/case-studies/
[93]www.chrisbrogan.com/five-starter-moves-for-introducing-social-media-into-your-organization/

first option. I'm going to step out and say that maybe a blog *isn't* a good first choice. Why? Because I think that blogs are fairly substantial steps and that an organization might feel really exposed if its first attempt at clearing its throat is an onstage a cappella moment in front of thousands.

Why not start with a tumbleblog or a posterous account? In fact, an organization could even do a stealth trial of the feel of blogging by doing a few throwaway tumbleblogs that *aren't* about the organization. Start with something that appeals to those who might be asked to blog. If they're into Texas hold 'em, cool. See if you can get them to post once every few days about poker.

Find some blogs that you'd want your organization to emulate in tone, style, and/or content, and subscribe to those in the reader, too (at this point, you might consider adding some folders to the reader, one for "listening" and one for "blogs"). Add a mix of related business blogs and maybe even some fun blogs to read, like poker blogs (to use my previous example).

Blogging is fun, empowering, and a great way to build the face of an organization, but it's also some people's version of standing naked onstage. Ease them into it. Give them a chance to get comfortable, then break out blogging.

INTERNAL, EXTERNAL, OR BOTH?

I advocate blogging inside the firewall (privately), as well as having a public-facing blog. The internal blogs make a great way to share and compare knowledge, and now that your company is full of professional RSS listeners, they can learn quickly the benefit of using a blog instead of e-mail for information sharing.

Back outside the firewall, facing the public space, your organization will want to be able to use its voice and talk about what matters to it. Some companies, such as Sun and Microsoft, have *tons* of company blogs, several written by engineers and people in the trenches. Blogging is *not* the responsibility of the marketing/communications team or the CEO. It's the responsibility of those who should be sharing their voices to open up the conversation to the company.

CHOICE OF PLATFORM

This isn't very important in the scheme of things, but I'll put in a plug for WordPress as being simple, configurable, and non-threatening. Hosting a copy of the application on your own site makes it a lot more configurable, but if that's an issue for IT reasons or because of some other roadblock, there's a free, hosted version, too.

Other platforms you can check out in the free and hosted camp are Blogger,[94] TypePad,[95] Vox,[96] and then about a gazillion others. As I said: It's not especially important, except in understanding the level of customization you want at your disposal.

---

[94]www.Blogger.com
[95]http://TypePad.com
[96]http://Vox.com

TOPICS OF CONVERSATION

If your organization has been reading other blogs that you've recommended, or blogs in your space, you should start to get a sense of what's important. From there, I'd recommend just trying it out. Post something. See what happens. See how people respond or not (comments should be enabled).

At www.chrisbrogan.com, I tend to talk about things on two levels: I start with a simple strategy and then finish with some actionable ideas. I call this notion "giving your ideas handles." Meaning, I want you to take what I share and apply it to your own needs, to make it your own. It's a great strategy for me, because it keeps people engaged, and it is, I hope, most often helpful.

There are tons of ways to start the conversation. Don't bog down on that. Just try something and see what happens. With that said, read what follows.

THINGS TO AVOID

Here are some easy land mines to avoid:

- It's okay to remove potty talk and unruly trolls from your blog's comments section. (Lots of people follow this rule: "If I wouldn't allow it in my living room, I won't allow it on my blog.")
- But *don't* delete comments that criticize you, provided the people stay civil. This is just begging for a brawl. It's considered in poor taste. Besides, that's one part of

blogging: understanding what people think of you. If you can't learn from your critics, where are you getting all your advice? Only from fans who rave about you?

- Don't repurpose other people's content without appropriate permissions. Learn about the Creative Commons and understand the difference between RSS making it easy for people to consume content and making it easy for people to steal content (a hot button with creative types).

- Don't just post press releases and marketing junk into a blog. No one will read them, and things will go "ghost town" quickly.

- Try to keep your blog open to more than just pitching yourself, your organization, and your services. It's your place, so you can do what you want, but if it's just a big fat ad, it will get boring, fast.

Sounds like there are lots of negatives to this blogging stuff, huh? Not exactly, but there *are* lots of ways to make a crummy first impression, and I wanted to cover all those.

WHAT YOU SHOULD GET FROM BLOGGING?

Blogging, when you're comfortable with it, is a great way to keep people in the loop about what matters to you. It's a great way to represent your organization. It's a wonderful way to share information back and forth, especially once you start learning from experiencing other people's blogs.

19

Five Starter Moves: Audio and Video

The Five Starter Moves series includes moving into audio and video. Is your organization is ready for that yet?

Getting your organization into more than just listening to the social sphere and blogging is not always the right move. Using these other media *can* be time-consuming, and the return on the effort is sometimes questionable. Yet audio and video connect people much more powerfully than just the printed word. It is with these tools that your clients, customers, partners, and colleagues can see the human behind the organization. This is at once scary and powerfully wonderful.

How Would You Use It?

Why would your company want to use audio and video? Are you hoping to build great viral videos like *Will It Blend?*[97] Are you hoping to share what's going on inside your organization? Maybe you are hoping to use it for recruiting, as promoted on Standout Jobs.[98]

---

[97]http://chrisbrogan.com/five-starter-moves-for-introducing-social-media-into-your-organization/
[98]http://standoutjobs.com/

For audio, there are lots of applications, including giving quick audio status messages, one-to-many, instead of using voice mail way (although you can sometimes collect audio from a mobile interface as well). You can use it to do conversational tips and advice.

In video, you can screencast on your products or share inside footage about how things are made (people love that stuff). You can share video status messages, use it as a tool for field engineers, and perhaps as a way to build relations between multilocation organizations.

WHICH TOOLS SHOULD YOU USE?

Some simple tools are in order here. There are complex ones aplenty, but here are some really good, simple, baby-step tools to help you get into creating audio and video for your organization.

Utterli

Utterli is a platform to enable sending audio, pictures, video, and text to the Web (to its community site, but it also can hook to your blog and post there simply, too). The audio messaging capability works on any phone that has the number 2 on the keypad. Technically, it works like leaving a voice mail, only it takes that message, digitizes it, and allows you to play it back as a digital file from your phone, Utterli's web site, or your blog.

Magnify Webcam

Magnify[99] offers a Flash-based webcam video-recording platform that is simple if you have a webcam to attach to a computer or if you want to upload movies you shot from another camera. I've used it for a few months and it works well.

12seconds.tv

For a video communications platform in a more conversational style, try 12seconds.tv. It's like instant messaging with video. There's a strong community there, and it might not be very business-focused just yet, but the tool works well, and the buzz about it is growing.

IS THIS A STARTER MOVE?

I'm not so sure. I think it's up to the organization, how you're thinking of using audio or video, and what you're thinking you can accomplish. I think the status messages idea for either audio or video makes for a great start, though. From there, you can explore, take small steps, and decide whether there's something else to consider.

---

[99]http://Magnify.net

20

Five Starter Moves: LinkedIn, Facebook, and Twitter

Companies are wondering how social networks will work for them and whether they should engage on those fronts. They've been told they should be doing it. They just aren't sure why or how. On one hand, some companies are thinking of these social networks as different channels for the same methods they have been trying in traditional marketing. On the other hand, some are just wondering how to get involved, which platforms will do what for them, and where to start. Here are some thoughts.

LinkedIn

LinkedIn is a fairly safe place to start for a business. It's targeted toward business professionals and is built mostly to be an online profile repository and a reputation management system. But it can be used for more.

LinkedIn is a great way to recruit into your business insofar as how your people write about themselves in their profiles. If your organization is on there, and people's profiles all seem to say good things about the organization, that's another way that folks can form an impression and interact with your company.

It's also a way to share knowledge and give an impression of your abilities. You can answer questions on LinkedIn. Sometimes this becomes an exercise in branding that can bode nicely for your company.

Facebook

I personally have mixed feelings about Facebook. At the least, it's a place where you as an individual can build a profile and have another touch point to the Web and to the potential of meeting new people with similar interests. Putting together a decent profile isn't especially difficult, but there are a few things I'd recommend:

- Use a picture that is more candid than posed.
- Consider which applications to add to your profile. They tell people a lot about you. Sure, you're going along with the crowd, but why?
- Join groups before you consider starting any. Participate.
- Evaluate the value of your efforts. Don't just stay there because people told you to be there.

What do you think? Are you using Facebook in a business way? Do you like it? Are you getting value?

Twitter

Ah, how do I describe Twitter? I have done so too many times to repeat myself in this part of the book. My business point about Twitter is this: Provided you are using Twitter conversationally and mixing and matching between sharing things about other people and maybe somewhat less about what you're doing, then it can be a useful tool for getting the message out.

I use Twitter a lot to ask questions. Some of my questions are just to promote conversation. Other times, I use it to direct attention to things that are useful or that matter, like social causes. Sometimes, I point Twitter toward my own stuff.

Social Networks in General

In general, social networks are useful for bringing about awareness, for meeting people outside the organization, and, as Rachel Happe from the Community Roundtable often says, for capturing unstructured information (e.g., status messages). Tread gently in using social networks, as the return on their use can be questionable. It's all a matter of engagement. *How* one engages is one thing. *Why* one engages is another. *What you get* out of the engagement is obviously the most important.

A Sample Social Media Toolkit

There are countless ways to get into the game with social media, but sometimes we get hung up on evaluating tools and thinking about which are the best for the job. We go further thinking about the variety of tools and why we'd use which ones for what, and then, next thing you know, the day is over and nothing's been done. Here are a few sample tools and what they can be used for, and from there, maybe some new ideas will spread. (Realize that these might be outdated soon after this book reaches the you.)

Quick note: I know, use, admire, and communicate with *lots* of providers of these tools. For every one of these categories, I could probably name between 4 and 16 more tools. If I didn't list your favorite, I probably still love you and your company. Maybe in the future I will publish a big fat list of resources.

The Quick List

For the sake of summary, let's list what's in our toolkit, and why, and then we'll go into detail after that:

- Listening tool: Google Reader
- Search tools: Technorati[100] and Google Blogsearch[101]
- Home base blog: WordPress.com or WordPress.org (to host your own)
- Scratch blog: Tumblr.com or Posterous.com
- Better reach: FeedBurner
- Mobile blogging: 12seconds.tv, Utterli, Qik
- Social conversation: Twitter
- Social profile: Facebook
- Business profile: LinkedIn

---

[100]http://Technorati.com
[101]http://Blogsearch.Google.com

- Social bookmarking: Del.icio.us
- Collaboration: PBwiki[102]
- Shared documents: Google Docs
- Instant messaging, Web-based: Meebo or Campfire[103]
- Photo sharing: Flickr or Zooomr[104]
- Video hosting: Blip.tv (also YouTube)

WHAT THEY ALL DO

Google Reader and the two search tools make it easy for you to set up a quick network of searches on topics, brands, company names, and whatever else you want to follow in your space. When I say "home base" blog, I think that in *most* cases, making your main web site a blog is preferable to something static. Why? Because it hints at recurring content. It fills search engines with things to think about.

A "scratch" blog might be one that you don't even publish to the outside world, but the beauty of Tumblr is that you can blurt out short text, audio, video, and other things to the site. I keep a few around for a few different purposes: one for private notes, and one for multimedia posts.

I use FeedBurner to improve the quality of my RSS feeds, to give people more options to subscribe[105] to my posts, and to provide some extra functionality.

---

[102]http://pbwiki.com

[103]http://Campfirenow.com

[104]http://Zooomr.com

[105]http://feedproxy.google.com/chrisbrogandotcom

Utterli is a simple tool you can use from *any* mobile device (the barrier to entry is whether or not it has the number 2), and post either audio, text, photos, or video. Qik[106] does live video streaming if your phone supports making movies.

Twitter allows for one-to-many messaging from multiple points (Web, IM, third-party app, or mobile device). It's also good for presence and for sharing quick status information.

Facebook actually does lots of things and is a full-featured social network; at the baseline, fill out a personal profile with lots of information about you and links back to your main site and/or your blog, and it will do a great job of helping people find you. Other features exist, including groups and several third-party applications. There are lots of things to explore there.

LinkedIn is a popular site for posting a summary of your current job role and responsibilities, as well as a work history. There is now a group feature there as well, and you can use this tool extensively to reach out and meet new colleagues in your field and prospective employees, and there are all sorts of other uses for such information, if you give it some thought.

I like Del.icio.us (pronounced "delicious") for social book-marking because it means my bookmarks are out on the Web, so I can access them from anywhere. It also means that I can add tags and other metadata to the bookmarks to improve the ways I search for them.

We've used wikis for collaboration projects, such as plan-ning an event (we built PodCamp on a wiki, and it's still running

---

[106]http://qik.com/

strong!), or sharing status information that might need to be changed by more than one person. There are tons of free wiki software projects out there. I think PBwiki is simple, flexible, and easy enough to share with others. The only tricky thing about explaining wikis to colleagues who aren't up to speed is the name itself. If you just say "collaborative web page" or some such, it's easier.

Google Docs works as a great replacement for sharing word processing and spreadsheet functions. It's free, secure, and makes for less file clutter, as you're sharing a link to a shared, common document instead of sending around various versions. Google Docs also has presentation software, though I haven't had much experience with it just yet.

Instant messaging isn't dead. There are still plenty of great business uses for quick one-to-one conversations. Meebo is a great tool because it lets you bridge several services at once (desktop apps that do the same thing are Adium for the Mac and Trillian for PC) and chat with people about quick-hit items.

Photo sharing and video hosting can be used in lots of ways. They make for richer interactions, add some dimension to the media you're making with your company, and give you an opportunity to express your story in different ways than straight text.

HOW YOU MIGHT USE THESE TOOLS

I won't go into each and every tool, but here is a quick rundown of some tools and how you can use them for business purposes:

- *Listening tools*. Understand how people react to your organization, follow your competitors' news stories, learn more about things that might impact your business.
- *Blogging*. Communicate your company's news, discuss the industry as a whole, share information and learning, respond to things you find while listening; use internally as a status platform.
- *Mobile tools and social conversation*. Use for status and presence information, visuals from field engineers, audible daily meeting messages.
- *Collaboration and shared documents*. Offer project plans, intention documents, status reports, meeting minutes, shared creative projects.
- *Instant messaging*. Use in meetings while virtual, back-channel during conference calls, quick integrated conversations.

PERSONAL USE

Lots of these tools are often explained as a way to communicate outward to lots of people, which is the way they are typically used, yet, as I explained earlier in my "scratch blogs" use, there are all these great tools to use for yourself as a creative type looking to capture information on the fly. Remember that tools have an obvious first use, but sometimes, they have a different use when applied to a different kind of problem. Don't lose sight of that option.

Social Media and Social Network Starting Points

Organizations have a lot to consider once they decide they want to jump into social networks and social media. There are many opportunities to slide off the rails, or worse, to let the effort fall into disarray. Here are some thoughts based on a question I received recently in an e-mail about guidelines, a toolbox, and how to grow a community.

START WITH THE INTENT

First, know what the intent of your social media and networks will be. Are you hoping to improve awareness and open communication about your organization? Are you looking to reach new markets and open channels for sales or membership or market adoption? Are you hoping to use these tools as collaboration platforms? Are you making informational products? Are you just virtualizing your watercooler?

Knowing your intent drives which path you take.

TREAT YOUR COMMUNITY LIKE ADULTS

Companies and organizations are most worried about how blogs and podcasts and wikis will be used. The truth is, most employee codes of conduct cover this related to e-mail use. It's not much different. Don't add another thousand rules about what should go on within the social networks, except insofar as what differences come with the medium. For example, don't bury people in what not to say. If you're a publicly traded company, have your bloggers add a disclaimer (e.g., "strictly my opinion"), remind them about the e-mail policy, and let it go.

A SAMPLE BLOGGING POLICY

If I were launching a social media program at a company, I'd hold a quick meeting in person. I'd mention the following:

- We're opening up blogging to the organization. Every one here is now invited to use our new blogging platform. Why do this? Because we think you're creative, intelligent people, and we want to give you a chance to share your ideas with a larger audience, inside and outside the organization.
- As this is public, just remember that we can't talk about company secrets, upcoming projects that aren't yet public, or anything that could impact our company's stock value.
- Within reason, you can say what you will about our publicly released products and services. If you're critical

of something, recommend solutions. Offer examples of improvements. We'd prefer it to be constructive. Use your judgment.

- When posting pictures or movies or music, understand that some materials may be copyrighted. For instance, just because you can see a picture on a Google Image Search or find it in Flickr doesn't mean you have the right to post it on your blog. We'll talk more about Creative Commons and some other resources later.

- Off-topic posts are fine. We don't expect every single post to be about the organization. We hope you'll talk about us from time to time, as our goal is showing our customers, vendors, and other stakeholders, as well as the community at large, that *you* are what makes our company amazing.

- Mentioning our competitors is fine. The world doesn't revolve around us (okay, we pretend it does!), and we know that some people do some aspects of what we do better. Don't rub our noses in it, but we get it.

- Deleting blog posts is considered bad etiquette on the Web. We won't do it here, unless something violates our privacy policies and/or our ethics policies. Posting hotties probably won't fly, but the occasional cute picture of your cat in a cowboy hat is okay. You're a real human, not a robot.

- Did we mention it'd be cool if you talked about us once in a while? Great!

- It's considered good etiquette to link to other great posts you read, and to comment on other blogs written by people you admire or want to engage in conversation.

- As for how often or how much is too much and things like that, around here, we measure you on your results at your primary function. If your work starts suffering on your way to becoming an A-list blogger, we'll have to adjust your expectations a little bit. Otherwise, use your judgment.

Something along those lines would be a good starting point for a blog policy, I think. Have you written a blog policy? What's *yours*?

ELEMENTS OF YOUR SOCIAL MEDIA PLATFORM

People are selling all kinds of technology for blogging, even though there are plenty of free and open-source platforms out there. Simple, hosted opportunities abound. Beyond that, there are some great new collaborative products, and *tons* of content management software companies make all flavors of solutions. Instead of recommending any specific platform, I'll point out some things to consider:

- Operating environments vary: Several content systems work on Linux platforms, using solely open source, and others are built for a Windows environment. If you're building the system in-house, consider what your IT team will be comfortable supporting. Or consider bypassing both camps entirely and build on a hosted environment out on the Web.

- Related to the last point, the more arcane or unknown the system, the less likely it will be for you to find support should the vendor and you fall out of love. Be wary of that.

- The content system should feature RSS feed support. This means that all the content can be exported via a specific protocol that allows people to view it in a reader or another application of their choice, and not just at the web site as a destination. (For me, systems that don't support RSS are showstoppers. You might have a different opinion.)

- The ability to post in a simple, visual manner (that would feel like using a tool like Microsoft Word) as well as the ability to post in HTML format is useful. I like writing in HTML, but others might prefer the comfort of the WYSIWYG tools.

- Media support is fairly standard these days, but should be considered. In a world where YouTube is no longer just skateboarding dogs, the ability to embed Flash video, as well as the ability to post MP3 and MOV files (among other types) would be important.

- Video has lots of added challenges. I strongly recommend a third-party hosting platform, then embedding a player instead of integrating to your platform. Yes, there are great platforms working inside the firewall, and there are some easy add-on video solutions, but if you're going to go heavy into video and aren't a production or media company, that part is probably best outsourced.

- Is mobile a priority? Applications such as Utterli, Tumblr, and others allow for mobile posting. Integrating input from more than one source would thereby also be important and of interest. Pay attention to how easy it is to import feeds and post into your media platform. This is one limitation that can be somewhat vexing later on.

- Backing up, exporting, importing, and some administrative functions are important to consider if you're going to put any serious data and effort into the platform. For example, I do full backups of the data on www .chrisbrogan.com every week, regardless of the fact that it's posted on a hosting system.

- Customization is important. If you can't make the platform look and feel like the rest of your presence, what's the point? Most systems accommodate for this rather well, permitting Cascading Style Sheet (CSS) support and other features, but make sure.

- Beyond this, there are lots of "your mileage may vary" opinions, but this should be a good start.

KEEPING A COMMUNITY ALIVE AND GROWING IT

I saved the hardest part for last. In that old Kevin Costner movie, *Field of Dreams,* the tagline/hook of the movie was a ghostly voice in the cornfields saying, "If you build it, they will come." Nothing is farther from the truth.

People's attention spans are frayed to their very edges. Work stresses are equally ramped up. The "shiny new thing" quotient on the Web is at its highest right now. So the odds of making a full, fat, rich, robust community that swells into the hundreds of thousands overnight is fairly slim. For every "overnight" success like Club Penguin for kids or Facebook for everyone else, there are tons of digital ghost towns out there. I'm not about to say that I know what the secret ingredient is, because if I did, I'd make my own network, get Microsoft and Google to bid me up to the billions, and retire to Newfoundland.

Here, instead, are some thoughts.

- Communities that have "something to do" do better. Want an example? Amazon. You can go there and review books, write comments, build wikis, and do a million other things around products you love. Another? Flickr. Go there and look at other people's photos, join groups, tag and comment, and make notes. Facebook? You could get lost in all the time-wasting applications or become deeply involved in all the groups there. Make sure there's something to do.

- Go outside the borders often. New communities grow by gently encouraging new immigrants. For example, if you're active on Twitter, you can occasionally point to posts on your new community. Not always. That quickly becomes boring. You can comment on other blogs that are similar to your group's intent and where you populate your URL (in most blogs, you enter your name, e-mail, and URL). Folks click on the URL of comments that seem interesting. (Don't spam!)

- Encourage more than you stifle. You want to see a community turn on their keepers? When sites go astray of their community-minded goals, bad things happen. Look at what happened[107] when the social news site Digg changed its algorithm a bit. It wasn't pretty. So be wary of how you interact with the community.

- Make it worthwhile for the community. If you're going to build a place for people to collaborate and share ideas and build content, be on the lookout for ways to give something to your community members for their efforts.

- Administrators are not community managers. Community managers exist out there who know all the great ways to engage people. Connie Bensen,[108] Jake McKee,[109] Jeremiah Owyang,[110] and a host of other great people are community types to their very bones. They know how to energize a community. Seek out a community manager to run the environment and make that his or her primary role. This is worth *tons* in the long run.

---

[107]www.nytimes.com/idg/IDG_002570DE00740E18002573DA005F4030 .html?ref=technology

[108]http://conniebensen.com/

[109]http://communityguy.com/

[110]http://web-strategist.com/blog

OTHER PEOPLE'S NETWORKS

Here is one consideration for when to build your own social network and when to use existing social networks: having an abundance of community members in your organization already versus seeking to grow a community. If it's the first scenario, then build a social network. If you're looking to grow from nothing, consider starting in other people's social networks.

I use both methods for my own interests. I think it's important to be part of the community at large, so I participate on Twitter, to a lesser extent on Facebook, and then in a variety of other places. My personal method is to focus on the people, not the platform, meaning that I'm not on Facebook because it's Facebook. I'm there because some of my friends and business colleagues are there. That's a popular Eric Rice[111] warning to social networks, too. He goes where his crowd is, not just to the new and shiny thing.

For you, it's mostly a question of whether you have the community in place and are looking to target those within your platform, offering them tools and resources to connect and cross-communicate. One of my favorite examples of this is FastCompany.com, which for a while turned its online property into a social network around its magazine's points of business instead of simply a rehash of its magazine. It's a bit more blended these days, but there are still many community features built in. Points go to USAToday.com for its effort, too.

---

[111]http://ericrice.com/

Is there a hybrid model? I think so. You can perhaps build a network and understand that it might be slow to grow, and then grow your community by participating in "outpost" areas like Facebook or Twitter or the other billion networks that are out there.

PEOPLE ARE THE CORE

At the core of this are people. Everything that has come before this doesn't work a lick until you understand the people you intend to reach, the people you hope will contribute, and the people who will share their time with you on all angles. If, for instance, you start a blogging platform at work, then complain that people are using it, they won't use it. If you build a social network dedicated to talking about how great your company or products are, that will get old really fast.

Do you know humankind's greatest need? The need to feel wanted. If you consider the incentives behind most people's actions in a given day (especially mean people), what's at the core of it is to feel that they're doing something important, interesting, and worthwhile. That has to be at the center of your motivations and perspective if you're launching a project like this. Make it worth it for the people, and they will participate.

NOW, JUST START

Analysis paralysis is a terrible thing. Just try something. Even if you launch a really small part of your project's intentions, now is the right time to try. What's holding you back?

If you want advice, or if you want to customize this information for your organization, I'm always available to talk more. I have a contact form at http://chrisbrogan.com/contact. Let me know what you need. I'm always happy to help.

What *Friends* and *Seinfeld* Teach You about Growing Your Audience

Back in the 1990s, NBC had this perfect little plan for its superpowered Thursday night lineup. It would run *Friends,* then some other show, then *Seinfeld,* and then some other show, then *ER*. In the "other show" slots, NBC would place its not-so-popular products that hadn't yet learned to stand on their own. They were incubator spots. And that's my recommendation to you if you're looking to grow your audience.

FIND YOUR *FRIENDS, SEINFELD, ER*

If you're a medium- or small-size blogger or podcaster, find the content that is most similar to what you're talking about.

Start commenting, contributing, and finding ways to augment instead of seeming like a cloned product. Look for the things others are *not* covering and make that your deeper specialty. (Side note: If you feel you're truly unique, that's either really awesome or it's going to stink for you.)

Don't latch on like a leech, but do see if you can at least establish a conversational relationship.

BE YOUR OWN SHOW

Essentially, TV shows that attempt crossovers suffer. So do comic books (ask any comic writer and most fans). Make sure you're your own product and that your product stands alone really well. The model at NBC was that the show in between *Friends* and *Seinfeld* either succeeded and graduated to its new date and time, or it went dead quickly.

THINK ABOUT THE LANDSCAPE

Consider how your blog improves someone's day. In fact, here's homework: Look at your blog as if it's a book on a shelf. Now, imagine that bookshelf is in Barnes & Noble (or in Chapters, for my Canadian friends) and that you have music, video, and other things to contend with.

Be holistic about this. Think about your audience's time. Are they reading, watching, consuming you and several other blogs? Or do they even have much time for blogs with work, TV, school, kids, spouses, and hobbies that don't involve keyboards

(I've heard some exist). How can you make your product *so good* that it becomes "appointment viewing?"

That's what you need to target.

The products I stick with, blogwise, are informational and deliver value repeatedly. The video blogs and Internet TV shows I like all hit me hard and keep me wanting more. In all cases, I feel like I'm learning, that there's very little deadweight in the output of the product, and that I'm getting the best return for my time spent.

You *must* think about your own stuff the same way.

LOOK FOR AUDIENCE CROSSOVER

I already mentioned that your product has to stand alone and that crossovers on TV and in comics stink, but what I didn't say and should is that *audience* crossover is magic. Wherever you can find ways to get a big product's audience to interact with you, it's good. Don't get onto someone else's blog and just pimp the hell out of your blog. That won't work. It just comes off as seeming way too self-serving. But it doesn't hurt to quickly write a follow-up topic that augments a blog whose audience might really love your stuff.

Product crossover is bad (usually). Audience crossover rocks. Know the difference.

ALWAYS SEEK TO ENGAGE

I've recently started a personal "side blog"[112] where I can do "lab" projects, where I can talk about me for my own sake.

---

[112]http://chrisunplugged.tumblr.com/

Why split it out? Only because my goal, first and foremost here, is to deliver value to *you,* and that means ruthlessly cutting some of what I feel isn't of value.

Yes, it's cool to know more about the people you read and experience, but pound for pound and bang for shelf space in my personal virtual store, I want you getting what you come here for, and I want to engage you.

I don't find telling you about my little Twitter experiments engaging—until they are.

FRIENDS AND SEINFELD MAY BE GONE

But the lessons NBC gave us live on. See if you can work some of this into your own media making, and let me know what you think. How does your product compare, compete, and complement other products out there? Have you thought about it much? What can you share?

24

Twitter Revisited

Twitter is the stupidest thing anyone could ever imagine inventing. If I said to you, "I've got an application that I want you to install that is addictive, time-consuming, cross-platform accessible, and otherwise as sprawling as kudzu," would you say yes? No. Of course not.

And yet, *Twitter single-handedly changed my 2007*. It added tons more connectivity to my universe. It's given me experiences I didn't have the year before. It's brought me new relationships of value with people who matter to my business life as well as personally.

There are tons of folks who have mixed opinions of Twitter and how to use it, why to use it, and so forth. Here's my take on how I use Twitter and/or how you might find some use in it, as well as some simple Twitter etiquette.

TWITTER IS A BUILD-IT-YOURSELF COMMUNITY

You show up with no friends, and the first thing you have to do is look around and see who you should add. Or you can dump your in-box into Twitter's machine and see if you know anyone. I often recommend this (adding your in-box), but *not* necessarily inviting everyone in your box to join if they haven't already. (Folks are starting to frown on that experience.)

However, there are some considerations before you jump in and add everyone. Here's something to consider from a guy with 103,000 or so people in my stream (circa October 2009):

- Adding everyone to your Twitter stream means there's more energy, more breadth of interest, but also less ability to focus on a smaller group of people who matter more to you than the others.

- Twitter is a conversation, not a broadcast. If you add lots of people, expect to try to talk back and forth with them, or lose steam fast.
- There's a lot of "noise" to go with most Twitter people's "signal." Choose people who talk about things that matter to you.
- Abandon all thoughts of Twitter being a professional marketing tool. It will have the occasional sway, but not as often as you need to make that worth it. (It's not meant for that purpose.)
- If all else fails, look for people you know and like, see who *they* have as friends, and add them.

TWITTER IS A GREAT PLACE TO SHARE IDEAS

It's a virtual watercooler, for sure. You can stand around, blather about the news, about your dinner, about the movie you saw last night, or something that matters more to you. The content is yours. And you can work out quickly what your friends on the service choose to talk about more often than not.

But it's not exactly the right place for a conversation. There are plenty of better resources for that, such as IM, or taking the conversation onto a blog, or even conversing in the real world. Don't look at Twitter as a great conversation place, especially once you have a lot of friends. Look at it as an idea bank, a place to gather information, to inspire new thoughts, or to see what your friends are doing.

TWITTER IS A GATEJUMPER

In the early 1990s, e-mail was a gatejumper. People would answer e-mail, even if they had no idea who you were. Then, somewhere in the late 1990s, blogs became the gatejumpers. People would interact with you if you commented on their blogs. Now? Twitter. Tomorrow? Not sure. It's getting really thin.

But, for some reason, Twitter has brought me into meaningful conversations offline with people I knew only through Twitter. My experience on Twitter really redefined my 2007, because it allowed me to communicate with some really great people, most of whom I'd not yet met in person but knew by way of their media.

I'm fond of saying that Twitter is the "director's commentary" for our media. It's in that form that I find Twitter to be a great gatejumper.

TWITTER IS THE MATRIX STREAM

There's a scene in *The Matrix* where Tank (or one of those *Matrix* types) explains that he can watch the patterns of data and see something fairly clearly. I use Twitter like that a lot. I use it like a big, smart computer. I ask Twitter questions (meaning all several thousand of you), and I get back answers.

If you choose to accumulate a whole lot of Twitter friends, expect to use Twitter more like a flowing stream than a one-on-one catch-up-with-your-friends tool. I rarely see my close friends rush by in the stream. Instead, I have to set up little ways to watch them, like using Seesmic Desktop[113] to set up groups and interact that way.

---

[113]http://seesmic.com

TWITTER ISN'T FOR EVERYONE

If you're a small business looking at Twitter as a way to grow your business, I'm not convinced that it'll be the right tool for the job. If you're a big business trying to build relationships, you'd better really consider your Twitter strategy. Don't be the business; be the human. We interact with humans. Yes, we know you want to talk about your business, but talk to us as humans. Here's a weird one. Ask *us* what *we're* up to, and mean it. Then, if we like you, we'll probably want to talk with you.

Think that's wasteful? Think how much money and time you're wasting in the fast-forwarding wars.

There are whole swaths of the world that Twitter isn't really meant to cover. That's okay. There are other tools. Remember, being a "me too" and joining just because some people use it is like deciding you have to learn how to throw a 95-mile-an-hour fastball because you like watching baseball.

Try it out if you want. See whether it works for you, and then decide what to do with it.

SOME TWITTER TIPS

Here are some specific ways to use Twitter that you might not have considered or that you might want to reconsider:

- Start with Search. Go to http://search.twitter.com and input words that pertain to your workplace, your product, your competitors, your locale—whatever you want to track. Learn who's talking about what on Twitter, and you'll immediately use it better than most people who start out.

- Consider a desktop client and a phone client. My personal preference is Seesmic Desktop, which requires Adobe AIR to run, or you can try TweetDeck.[114] I'm not printing the phone number here, because it feels like a dozen new Twitter iPhone and Droid apps come out every week, and platforms like BlackBerry and Palm are catching up, too.

- If you want to promote your blog or podcast, at least try to do it conversationally. Ask people what they think about global warming as it applies to methane release on farms, and share the link. Don't just blurt out your podcast URL.

- If you want to build real friends in Twitter, pay attention to who uses lots of @ replies, and see how they interact with others. Some folks use Twitter like a bullhorn, and others use it like a walkie-talkie.

- If you want to use Twitter to meet new business colleagues, do what you'd do in other social media spaces: Learn more about them. Follow their links. Read their blogs. Get to know them. Don't just pounce all over them. It's easy to unfollow people in this space.

- Try this. Instead of "What are you doing?" try asking "What has your attention?" I find the answer is often more useful to others.

- Do your best to promote other people on Twitter instead of talking only about you and your things. If you find the good stuff, share the good stuff.

---

[114]www.TweetDeck.com

Case Study: For Those Who Pea on Social Media

Mainstream media thinks about social media: whether to crush it, whether to join it, whether to just ignore it. Marketers wonder whether they should use it as a new way to reach customers. Oh, maybe social media is about peas. Bear with me.

Susan Reynolds Pea'd Herself

To set the stage, Susan Reynolds[115] is an artist, a creative soul, and I met her earlier in 2007 via Twitter. She is part of the more "social" side of Twitter, keeping up with Ann Ohio and the gang. I know that Susan also gets into Second Life and that circle.

Only, one day, she learned that she had breast cancer. It all went fast, and the doctors gave her the big once-over. And after "a full afternoon of multiple stab wounds," as she puts it,[116] Susan learned that putting ice on her chest would help with the bleeding and the swelling and the pain.

Suddenly, Twitter was all about peas. Let me explain.

---

[115]http://susanreynolds.blogs.com/
[116]http://susanreynolds.blogs.com/boobsonice/2007/12/whats-with-the.html

SOCIAL MEDIA ISN'T JUST CHATTER

The Frozen Pea Fund[117] started Friday, December 21, 2007, to raise money for breast cancer research in Susan's name. Its a message was spread by Robert Scoble,[118] Shel Israel,[119] Jon Swanson,[120] and Connie Reece,[121] to name just a few.

People like Laura Fitton and Kosso set up a group Twitter feed,[122] and C. C. Chapman set up TwitterPeas.[123] Overall, it's a huge effort by lots of people to raise awareness of the campaign.

And this is to support a friend lots of us haven't even met in person. Yet the effort did lots to raise Susan's spirits, raising money, bringing even more attention via this new medium to something that was important and world-affecting, and it was definitely a project that spread virally. I doubt anyone would call it a failure, and instead, it's frequently referenced as a role model project for many other causes brought to Twitter over the years since.

---

[117]https://frozenpeafund.pbworks.com
[118]http://scobleizer.com/2007/12/18/davos-question-how-to-improve-the-world-my-answer-peas/
[119]http://redcouch.typepad.com/weblog/2007/12/susan-reynolds.html
[120]http://levite.wordpress.com/2007/12/20/i-hate-peas/
[121]http://everydotconnects.com/2007/12/20/community-vs-cancer/
[122]http://twitter.com/peaple
[123]http://twitterpeas.com/

SHRUG IT OFF IF YOU WANT

We're over here sending people to college,[124] supporting other cancer fund-raising programs,[125] microlending,[126] and joining plenty of other nifty causes that are helping real human beings.

Social media is a lot more than blogging, podcasting, and social networks. It's effective at reaching the people beyond the keyboards and microphones and connecting them to important things.

26

Basic Business Blogging Suggestions

You've decided you're going to take the recommendations of the office evangelist and start writing a blog. The word still bothers you, but you've been told that it's just like a newsletter or an article for a magazine, only faster and online. What comes next? How should you approach it? What will make the

---

[124]http://beth.typepad.com/beths_blog/2007/10/twitter-chris-b.html
[125]http://socialhoneycomb.com/dance-benefit
[126]http://kiva.org/

difference between a blog that people read and a blog that people ridicule? Here are some basic ideas and suggestions. None of these are rules. There are a hundred ways to do things.

ABOVE ALL ELSE, BE HUMAN

People read blogs (okay, we could argue that Google *also* reads your blog, but let's save that for another time). To that end, present yourself as a *human*. Write from a first-person perspective (use "I"), and write as if you're telling *me* something, not a faceless mass.

Also, be attentive to people's attention constraints.

COMMENTING IS JUST AS IMPORTANT

Remember to visit other blogs in the space and comment on stories and posts that appeal to you. Do *not* be "that guy" or "that girl" and reference yourself and your company in all these comments. Instead, be sure to seem human and comment on things that interest you. Commenting *matters,* and we know if you're part of our community by how and where you comment.

BLOGGING POLICIES

Your blogging policy shouldn't be any more complex than your e-mail policy. Look over your company's policy documents and see whether you can replace the term *e-mail* with *blog* and *blogging*. If the answer is yes and it makes sense, that's probably fine. It should go without saying that company strategy as well as financial data is not especially good to put on blogs.

If you *must* have some kind of policy in place whereby more than one set of hands has to touch a blog post, keep it simple. Anything more than two sets of eyes beyond the author, and I believe you've already killed people's interest in blogging.

DOES THIS TIE TO STRATEGY AT ALL?

Remember that your business blog has more requirements than a personal blog. Why did you start it in the first place? What's the *goal* of the blog? What are you hoping to do with it? Think this through and check your efforts against your goal regularly. If you can set up metrics of any kind, these might help.

For instance, if your goal is engagement, measure number of comments, Web hits, RSS subscribers, inbound links, and a few other criteria. But if your goal is customer service, maybe the blog itself isn't measured so much as overall sentiment in the marketplace.

My point, simply, is to pay attention to the strategy behind why you've bothered blogging in the first place.

PLATFORMS AREN'T *THAT* IMPORTANT

But you should consider whether the blogging platform you're using is easy enough to keep it enjoyable, whether it has RSS subscription capabilities, tagging, the ability to add plug-ins and external code, and a few other details that I'm happy to share, if this is a big concern.

MIX IT UP

We don't want to read *only* about your company, your product, and you. We want your take on the industry at large, on events that might resonate with us outside of your organization, on other forces that might impact our relationship with you and your products. Try to have that in mind when you write. Yes, it's a blog for your company, but it's also a source of information, and as such has to reflect the world around us.

DON'T SELL, BUT DON'T BE SHY

A blog isn't about the hard sell. Let's accept that. Yes, we'll be suggestive. Yes, we'll be persuasive. We'll give you tastes of what you might receive if you buy the whole deal, but if it's just a place for selling, we're not reading. It's the starting point of a call to action of what you're selling next.

There has to be passion and interest and information flowing through there. Sure, you can help us find where to buy things. But maybe try to mix it up a bit. Don't pretend you're *not* selling, because that can seem awkward, too, but if you can, consider the last few posts you've written and see whether it's time to sell to us again.

BUILD A WORK FLOW

The mood to blog might not always strike you. It might be helpful to keep a notepad file of topics and ideas so that you can tap into these when you have a moment. Also, don't be afraid to write into a text file and then dump it into your blog software when it's all finished. This will enable you to write anywhere, with or without the Web, when you have a moment. (Note: There are plenty of great tools for this as well, including Windows Live Writer for PC and Mars Edit for the Mac.)

Another trick to building a good blogging flow is to have a good blog reading habit. Use a tool like Google Reader and subscribe to sites and relevant searches that will keep you in quality posts.

LINK OUT

We pay attention to where you link. If every link in your blog is to your own stuff, we discount you as self-referential. Consider pointing out other great posts in your space, and give adequate links and credit. Don't sell the store, but make sure you're building a healthy linking habit. Otherwise, links will rarely flow inward as well.

FREQUENCY IS HOW OFTEN YOU HAVE VALUE TO ADD

If you blog on a monthly basis, your traffic will likely be dismal—unless you're Donald Trump, and then I imagine you'd pull it off. For the rest of us, try to stick to blogging weekly at worst and daily at best. Don't feel frustrated if you can't blog daily right away. Blogging takes practice, and it can sometimes fall to the bottom of our priority list (as it should). But if you build a decent work flow, this effort should become more natural over time.

PAY ATTENTION TO DESIGN

I wrote recently about blog design,[127] so I won't reinvent the wheel, but in brief, make sure you have easy-to-use contact information on the blog. Put up a very human "About" page, including information on the blog's author as well as the company you serve. We *know* it's a company blog. We want to know about *you*, too. Finally, make sure the blog has all the social sharing tools built into it, such that people can bookmark sites easily, share in popular places, and provide this information easily to others.

ENCOURAGE CONVERSATION

How do you build blog posts that last and add value? You encourage conversation. One way that I often do this is by asking questions of the people who read this blog. It's a great way to tap the expertise of the people in your space. No experts in the crowd? Then consider writing your posts in such a way that your most likely audience will have *something* upon which to comment and add their own value. Making a post too rock-solid is just an invitation to have nothing said about it after the fact.

---

[127]www.chrisbrogan.com/make-your-blog-design-work-for-you/

A Sample Blogging Work Flow

Your company has decided to launch a blog, and you're the lucky blogger. Maybe you've even asked for this pleasure, suggested it to the boss yourself. Only now you have to deliver, and you have to stay consistent. It's not always easy to keep up a steady blogging pace, and there are days when you might run into a roadblock or two that might keep you from delivering on your schedule. Here are some ideas about how to build and maintain a steady blogging rhythm, be it for your personal blog or your business blog. We cover goals, tasks, tools, and some bonus secrets.

GOALS OF YOUR BLOG POSTS

Blogging with a purpose helps you stay consistent. My blog, for example, is dedicated to equipping you with strategy, tools, and knowledge, so that you can go off and do useful things with social media and networking software. That's the main goal of the blog overall. Secondary goals are to maintain a presence in your mind, should you have business needs. Another goal would be to stay in the habit of writing, and working at improving my writing. Those are goals for my blog.

Goals for my blog *posts* (versus goals for the blog overall) are different from post to post. In addition to the previously stated ideas, here are some ways you might use specific posts:

- *Find prospects.* Most of my posts are helpful to you, but also spark an itch inside my prospective clients (either for speaking or detailed execution and consulting). This isn't an accident. I write for my clients as well as for you.
- *Seek link traffic.* I write certain posts (like anything with a big number) with a secondary goal of deriving links from you to the story. Why? Because that tells Google and Technorati that I'm doing good things over here, and that matters to how my blog is found.
- *Seek advice.* I often write posts in which I ask for your opinion. Why have a blog if you can't start conversations?
- *Establish thought leadership.* When I write about something far removed from what others are blogging about, it's to show you that I'm not a "me too" blogger.
- *Promote something interesting.* This might be people, software, or events. One point about promotion posts versus other kinds: If you're looking for comments, promotion posts rarely draw them.
- *Link love to others.* Sometimes, I want to give other people the spotlight, or point out good writing elsewhere. It's important to keep that in mind. Linking out promotes linking in.

BLOGGING TASKS

The *frequency* of blog posts you choose is important. Offering many posts per day is great, if you can keep it up. Once a day is probably ideal (but not as easy as it seems). Once every two or three days means your readers won't know what to expect. Once a week might be enough, depending on how niche-targeted your blog is and how authoritative you are to begin with. But no matter what you decide, make the decision and stick with the schedule. Within that schedule, here are some potential tasks to consider doing for every post:

- *Read material first.* Use your RSS reader to see what else is being talked about—in your industry, in your vertical, on friends' blogs, and most important, from fringe places that aren't related to you or your industry.
- *Compose a blog post.* If there's research and links involved, open a notepad file to keep track of the links you're intending to put in the post or sources of the data you're collecting.
- *Consider pictures.* Using pictures makes the posts pop. You can use Flickr photos marked with Creative Commons licensing, provided you cite the source of the original photo and provide a link. Read more about this at http://flickr.com/creativecommons, Flickr's Creative Commons site. There are other places for photos. Feel free to leave your other sources in the comments section at http://chrisbrogan.com/comments-from-101.

- *Tag your posts.* If your blogging software doesn't have tags built in, consider seeking a plug-in or at least having a few scripted copy/paste details of tags you can add to the bottom of every post. Tags are important for searchability, for getting the occasional new reader who finds you via your metadata.

- *Announce your best posts.* If I have a post I'm really proud of and think works well, I'll send a link to it via Twitter, usually summing up what I'm talking about before the URL. I might also send info about it via Facebook, via LinkedIn's status line, and/or via similar venues.

- *Occasionally, bookmark it, too.* If I'm *really* pleased by a post and want it to have legs, I'll share it in Google Reader's shared items (which sends it to other places), Stumble[128] it, and I might even Digg[129] it, too. If you do this kind of thing, be sure to Digg and Stumble and bookmark other people's stuff, too, when it's merited, so that you don't seem like a perpetual self-promoter. I do my best to maintain a balance. Hopefully, that shows through.

- *Check traffic and logs.* As the day goes on, check your stats reader of choice to see if the blog is having any kind of impact. If you have a decent ego surfing[130] mechanism set up, also see who's blogged about your post, and try

---

[128]www.Stumbleupon.com

[129]http://Digg.com

[130]www.chrisbrogan.com/social-media-power-secret-listening/

to add some value back to their write-up. Don't just drop by and say thanks. (Further note: Don't go crazy checking your blog stats. They're just a way to measure how people are responding to your posts.)

- *Get off your blog and comment elsewhere.* Make sure you're taking the time to comment on at least five blogs a day. Whenever you're going to bother posting and putting out new material, others are doing the same. Be sure to respect them and give them comments and feedback whenever you feel it's appropriate.

TOOLS

When you decide you have to maintain a blogging rhythm, regardless of whether you're doing this for business or your personal blogging goals, there are some important tools that you should consider. If you're going to get into a flow, here are the tools you should have on hand:

- *RSS reader.* I prefer Google Reader above all others because of several features, including its ability to rapidly scroll through information in list view, its search capabilities, its sharing capabilities (make your friends work for you), and all the other options. Starting your blogging habit by having a good blog consumption habit is the only way to fly.
- *Picnik*[131]. If you need free, easy, Web-based photo editing to make interesting pictures, check out Picnik. I find

---

[131]www.Picnik.com

this tool very useful in sprucing up my pictures. If you use it to edit other people's photos, be sure to check the permissions to see whether you *can* edit their images.

- *Skitch.*[132] Skitch is a screen capturing tool for the Mac that's very useful, and it has all kinds of built-in goodies.
- *Twitter search*. There's always something interesting to find in Twitter search.
- *Alltop.*[133] I get a lot of ideas by browsing categories in Alltop, an online magazine rack, from sources that aren't my own vertical. I get fertilizer for my seeds of thought this way.
- *Calendar*. Here's one. If you use a calendar (e.g., Google Calendar), you can make a new calendar to show what you've written about and what you plan to write about. This is called an *editorial calendar,* and it helps you keep your writing on a decent tack. Thus, if you intend to have two interviews a month and five product reviews, as well as a weekly check-in with some project, you can be sure to track all this in a calendar.
- *Notepad or text edit*. I write my blog posts in a plain text file so that I never lose a post to a bad Internet connection. Further, if I have a few moments (e.g., if I'm on a horrible conference call), I can jot notes—and occasionally write entire posts while offline. I do this a lot at airports, bookstores, and other places where the access to the Internet isn't a given.

---

[132]http://Skitch.com
[133]www.Alltop.com

THE BONUS ROUND

I guess in some ways, I should have started with this. First, if you're not reading Copyblogger,[134] you're missing some of the best advice on what to write and how to write it. Brian Clark and team (he has many guest writers!) keep a decent pace of giving you writing ideas and inspiration. Now, let's talk about some more ideas that will keep you going with blogging material:

- *Go to the grocery store.* There are more headlines and interesting ways of saying things right there in your face at the checkout counter than you'll likely come up with on your own. (I love this tip from Copyblogger.)
- *See what makes the front page of* Digg.com *(or your industry's most likely haunt).* Learning by emulating is an important blogging skill. Don't be a clone, but if you pick up some tricks from writers you come to admire, all the better.
- *Don't forget other media.* When using YouTube, Slide-Share, and other places full of free and interesting content, don't forget to give people a taste of video and audio to go along with your text and photo posts. In fact, be willing to mix it up often, or on a schedule, so that people get a sense of all the ways you can keep them informed and entertained.
- *Schedule posts.* This is my all-time favorite piece of advice. If you can, write more than one post at any given sitting.

---

[134]http://copyblogger.com/

Take the second post, especially if it's not time-specific information, and schedule it for the next day. If you do this repeatedly, you can build up quite a store of posts and never miss a day (or whatever your schedule is) due to a random issue. Note: You can usually reschedule things, in case the mood strikes, or news breaks, or the like. You shouldn't feel pinned down by this so much as *liberated,* for all the last-minute conflicts this will help you avoid.

Do what you need to do to feel comfortable with starting a blogging habit. Hopefully, this will give you some meat to go on.

28

If You Intend to Blog Seriously

Blogs are not traditional media, and bloggers are not journalists. Unless they are. But it's not a requirement. A blog is software. It's something one puts up on the Web to capture and disseminate information, of whatever type one wishes, and thus, if anyone tells you that you're doing it wrong, that's just silly. There aren't very many wrong ways to do it (except for illegal things, like stealing from others). And yet . . .

If you're going to blog seriously, keep in mind the following:

- Consider the goals and value of your posts. Are you adding to a body of work? Are you blogging to educate, to inform, to deliver some value?
- Facts do matter. If you're stating opinions, stress that they're opinions. If you're claiming a fact, try to cite sources. (I tend to state mostly opinions.)
- Remember that defamation is still a potentially legal issue.
- You can always ask questions *before* you blog (a novel idea, I know).
- Brevity matters. I know that I blog about this often. I see a number of posts where one has to wade through to try to decipher the salient points (often my own).
- Disclosure is key. If you're doing something to make money, if you have a business relationship with an organization that you're writing about, if there's anything that might potentially change the way something is perceived were it be to be measured against what you wrote, it's better to disclose that.
- Link when you're mentioning other sites or information that have links. It's good manners. It's the way the Web works. It's more resources. Linking only to yourself says something about you (and it's not flattering).
- Review the body of your work every 10 posts or so. Are you improving?

- Review the body of your work every 30 posts or so against the most recent. Are you repeating?
- Review the body of your work against five other blogs in your space. Are you an echo?
- Ask yourself *why* you're posting what you're posting. Pretend you're the reader. Is this worth his or her time?
- What else could you be doing with your blog to add value to your core community?

There are lots of reasons to be blogging: to capture your thoughts, to share moments, to build relationships, to establish thought leadership, to sell electric toothbrushes, whatever. None of them are especially wrong. But if you're going to blog with the perspective that you are a professional, give it your best. Your audience deserves it.

29

Performance and Your Audience: Blogging Tips

Performance. When you blog or podcast or record a video, it is an opportunity for a performance, a presentation, a distilled and distinct package of information. It is your chance to connect with your audience and deliver something of value. It is an obligation and a pact.

It's fine to use these tools for conversation, but consider your audience. Think about how little time they have in a day. Think about the places where they will be spending their time.

BE BRIEF

Can you say it faster? Do so.

APPEAL TO THEIR SENSE OF SELF

Can you tell a story? Will the story help your audience think of themselves? Will your words bring *their* minds awake?

BE PREPARED

It's not pressure to write good posts. It's not difficult to come up with topics for your podcast. It's your choice as a producer of good content. Think ahead. Keep a notepad file somewhere for ideas to use later, when you're stuck. Record a few extra "evergreen" bits to dispense at times you would otherwise come up short.

BE RESPECTFUL

Your audience is brilliant. You sometimes know something they don't. But treat them as though they are masterful and brilliant, as though you're just sharing this information in case they want to brush up. You're not a god. You're a communicator.

BE CONVERSATIONAL (YET CONCISE)

Talk as if you're addressing humans. I write as if you and I are having a conversation. Yet I try to keep things tight. I don't fret over it. I practice by posting once or twice a day. You can do the same.

PERFORMANCE

You're on a stage. You are creating stories. No matter how you view your blogging and podcasting, that's what you're doing. When you cook up that next MS PowerPoint deck for a meeting, think about that, too. It's the same thing, sliced differently. There's no reason to treat it differently.

What are some of your tips and advice? How do you treat your audience? When has it worked best for you?

Some Tips to Fine-Tune Your Blog

Blogging can be something one does for personal reasons, and if that's you, feel free to disregard all that I'm about to share with you. If, however, you're hoping that your blog's message has an impact on the community that matters to you, here are some ideas for tuning up your blog.

Some of this information is technical in nature. Don't tune it out right away because of that. Take notes on the parts you want to pursue, and then, if you can't do it by yourself, put up a quick ad on Craigslist for someone to tweak your blog. It would probably cost no more than $100 to do this stuff.

SOME BASICS

With millions and millions of blogs to read, our aggregate attention is fractured by competing attractions. As a blogger, you want to capture your audience early, give them value, give them extras, and send them on their way with a means to refer back to you, should they wish. Here are some tips and ideas for that:

- *Write really good titles.* Copyblogger always has good ideas on this.[135] A title that catches someone's attention, that is Google-friendly, or that describes things clearly will probably go a long way toward drawing people to your work. (By the way, this is technical, but set your titles in your blog posts to show the words of the post, not a page number or other weird random data. It helps Google, and that helps you.)

- *Chunk up your paragraphs.* If someone sees a big field of text, he or she will be less likely to dig in and read it. Try breaking things up visually by using subheaders, images, and other visual cues.

---

[135]www.copyblogger.com/clever-vs-descriptive-headlines-which-works-better/

- *Have a good "About" page.* Make sure people know *who* writes the blog. Blogging is a medium that helps build relationships, and the relationship between a writer and his or her readers can be very personal.

- *Brevity is your friend.* Cut unnecessary words and sentences from your piece. The more concise and useful your posts, the more return traffic you should expect.

- *Answer comments often.* As often as you can, dig into your comments section and answer back. I got this advice from Bryan Person,[136] and when I heed it, my blog flourishes. When I don't get a chance to respond to comments, posts fade away faster.

- *Use FeedBurner for RSS.* Actually, use lots of tools to extend the reach of your blog. But FeedBurner, in particular, adds all kinds of valuable things to a standard RSS feed. You can add a "subscribe by mail" box to your blog. You can republish your feed in other formats. You can extend it out in *lots* of good ways.

SOME NITPICKY PARTS

The following are my own personal gripes and opinions, and, of all of my advice on blogging, consider this to be mostly my own personal views—which you don't have to go along with it if you don't want.

---

[136]http://bryper.com/

I don't like too many widgets, buttons, or add-ons on the sidebar of a blog. It just messes up the design and confuses the "call to action" of the blog.

MORE THINGS TO CONSIDER

Here's a quick list of things to consider about the overall ecosystem of blogging. These are also personal opinions, but I'll say that I've seen lots of good return in my life from these efforts.

- Read lots of good things (listen and watch lots of good podcasts and video blogs). Great stuff coming *in* makes for good thoughts going *out*.
- Link to great blog posts elsewhere, but try to add something to the conversation. People respond better to your riffing on someone's original idea than they do when you just point out a pile of links.
- Whenever you can, share resources that you discover, whether they are great people or great pieces of information. Consider using a social bookmarking tool such as Del.icio.us, Clipmarks, or a Tumble blog.
- Comment frequently on other people's blogs. Be part of the conversation, not just someone throwing posts out into the world.
- Consider building a blogroll of blogs you like. (I used to have a Rockstars page for this.) Or at least consider a widget for your shared items from Google Reader.
- Don't feel as though you have to blog daily. Instead, blog when you have a good idea worth sharing.

SOME ANALYSIS TOOLS

How will you know what you want to fix if you don't know how your blog is being used and seen? The shiny graphic you see up top comes from a service called CrazyEgg.[137] (A tip of the hat to Cory at Strike 3 Designs for sharing it with me.) By adding just a simple snip of code to your blog, CrazyEgg can tell you who's clicking where on your site. It's a really interesting tool with lots of visualization methods built in. You can use a free version to start, then sign up for CrazyEgg's subscription model, which isn't that expensive, if you have more serious needs in mind.

If you want to go a little deeper in checking who's doing what with your site, I also recommend using Google Analytics,[138] which will give you granular details about who's coming from where, what people are doing, and tons more. Other good statistical information comes from FeedBurner and similar places, if you use them for your RSS subscriptions, and by using tools such as Website Grader,[139] which gave me *tons* of information on how to improve my blog technically.

SOME HOPE THAT YOU BLOG FROM YOUR HEART

Even if you're a professional blogger looking to make a living from your blog, consider blogging from the point of view

---

[137]http://crazyegg.com
[138]http://Analytics.Google.com
[139]http://Website Grader.com

of your passionate observations. Lots of people can report the facts, and plenty of people have covered lots of different areas of interest with factual blogs. But finding people who are truly creating interesting original content is rare.

For every 10 pundits, we should have an original thinker.

If you can, contribute new thoughts, different takes, and mash-up ideas to the mix. Take something you've read or heard or seen from two different perspectives and mash them into a new thought. Share something from your life. Share what matters most to you, mixed with how it might be helpful and of interest to others. Put out crazy ideas. Put out heartfelt ideas. Deliver from your heart and soul, and it will show through. A great example of this is Jon Swanson's Levite blog.[140]

31

How to Create Business from a Blog

First, let's agree that there are many ways to create business from a blog. I'll cover a handful to start. You're very welcome

---

[140]http://levite.wordpress.com

to share more advice and ideas in the comments section on my site at http://chrisbrogan.com/comments-from-101.

STRAIGHTFORWARD SALES

Blogs are a wonderful piece of software to use as a home base for several kinds of web site projects. For example, Chris Pearson[141] used a WordPress blog to build his DIYthemes site.[142] There, he's selling a beautiful theme called Thesis.[143] That's one way to create business from a blog: a simple sales platform.

AFFILIATE MARKETING

Another way is through affiliate marketing. For example, go back and hover your mouse over the URL for the two links to Chris's latest project. You should see this: http://diythemes .com?a_aid=t4ag3. That part after the ? is an *affiliate code*. Some sites don't really divulge that they're doing affiliate marketing. Others make disclosure very vital. Now that you know what to look for, you might check other blogs you read and see when they're slipping you an affiliate tag here and there. (In my case, I fully disclose all such relationships on my About page of my blog—see http://chrisbrogan.com/about.)

Want to learn more about affiliate marketing? I've been reading ReveNews,[144] a blog about the space, and I attend the

---

[141]http://pearsonified.com/

[142]http://Diythemes.com

[143]http://diythemes.com/?a_aid=t4ag3

[144]www.ReveNews.com

Affiliate Summit[145] to learn more from the leaders in the game.

LEAD GENERATION

Blogs are a great way to establish thought leadership and, further, to encourage lead generation. For instance, much of my blog is about sharing with the world at large what I know about social media and how it might apply to your business. My primary goal is to share with you as much information as I possibly can, so that you can likely run off and solve most things on your own.

My secondary goal is to encourage you to contact me if you have business needs. I work with CrossTech Partners to help me fulfill larger projects (building market relationship management platforms, etc.). This blog often starts conversations with people who need next-step help. And that's great. It's another value, another way to create business from a blog.

A great person who gives abundantly with her blog is Liz Strauss.[146] She derives some amount of leads from her thoughtful and meaningful efforts, too.

CONTENT MARKETING

He could tell you this every day, but Brian Clark[147] has been praising the value of content marketing since 2006. This is

---

[145]www.affiliatesummit.com

[146]http://successful-blog.com/

[147]http://copyblogger.com/

basically how the Financial Aid Podcast[148] brought millions in revenue to Christopher S. Penn's Student Loan Network.[149] There's nothing shady about it. Chris creates great podcasts and blog posts and uses the trust earned through information sharing and helping others as one way to drive sales of his primary product: student loans. He's the only student loan guy I know who is profiled by *Business Week*, the *Wall Street Journal*, and all kinds of other press.

See also Gary Vaynerchuk,[150] the only wine seller I know who has a Hollywood agent. He's *that* cool.

Content marketing essentially means providing useful and interesting content with the goal that this work leads to a sale. To me, this is "the thing" right now. If I were looking to build even more business, and I might just do so, I'd blend content marketing with a mix of my own products, and perhaps some well-chosen affiliate opportunities, and start from there.

By the way, content marketing has the added benefit of helping you with organic search engine optimization, meaning that it helps people more easily find the things they're searching for.

OTHER OPPORTUNITIES

There are lots of other ways to make money from a blog. I'm definitely not qualified to talk about search marketing, for

---

[148]http://FinancialAidPodcast.com
[149]http://studentloannetwork.com/
[150]http://tv.winelibrary.com/

instance, but an article by Paul J. Bruemmer[151] provides a useful starting point. There are also projects like Ted Murphy's IZEA, which covers pay-per-post and SocialSpark.[152] I'm not versed enough to talk about any of these, but you can swing by the IZEA blog.[153]

The Web is an interesting place to make money these days, and there are many ways to take a swing at it. Be open about what you're doing. Be helpful. Offer value. And maybe something will come of it for you.

Update: Here's a plug for Darren Rowse[154] and Chris Garrett's[155] book, *ProBlogger: Secrets for Blogging Your Way to a Six-Figure Income.*

YOUR IDEAS

If you have some other great ideas for creating business from a blog, let's talk about them in the comments section at http://chrisbrogan.com/comments-from-101. Some will be promoted to the main post via updates, so please fill out your URL when you comment, so I can give you credit if I use it in the post.

What do you think?

---

[151]http://searchengineland.com/080702-071343.php

[152]http://socialspark.com/

[153]http://community.izea.com/blog/

[154]http://problogger.net/

[155]http://chrisg.com/

50 Blog Topics Marketers Could Write for Their Companies

You've started a company blog. What comes next? It's not like someone gives you blog topics and an editorial calendar and suggests which one to post first. Well, I'm here to help. As part of my ongoing desire to see you pick up these social media tools for yourself and change the future of your business, here are 50 blog topics marketers could write for their companies. (Feel free to repost them, but please link back to www.chrisbrogan.com.) Oh, and if some of these don't fit exactly, think creatively about whether you could adapt them.

50 BLOG TOPICS FOR MARKETERS

1. How to get the most from our customer service department.
2. The best way to recommend an improvement to our product or service.
3. Podcast—complete installation instructions in audio and video.
4. What would you like to see in next year's catalog?

5. Our favorite projects over the coming months.

6. Some tricks that might keep you from needing support.

7. Upcoming coupons and offers for the next two weeks.

8. We want to talk. How should we contact you? Where?

9. Choose our product's price.

10. Five tips for getting more from your _____.

11. A little bit about us.

12. A walk in our neighborhood.

13. Photos from our community meetup.

14. What goes into our decision process.

15. Video—a tour of the plant, a day in the life of your product.

16. What it's like to work for our company.

17. We support these causes, and here's why.

18. The next two years: how we grow with you.

19. We want to come to work with you (and learn how we can help)!

20. Giving back to the community: our plan.

21. What we worry about over the coming year.

22. How we handle your disputes or complaints.

23. Can you recommend a better process for this?

24. Sometimes, we have to say no.

25. Your call is important to us. We'll tell you *how* important.

26. We're sorry, and here's how we'll handle things next time.

27. Report from our independent community review board.

28. How to close out your account with us. (Imagine how risky this is!)

29. The economy is piling up costs, and we have to share the burden.

30. Understanding what went wrong.

31. Birthday announcements for August. (Imagine listing your customers' names on a birthday calendar.)

32. Fourteen ways to customize your _____.
33. Why we like our competitor's product better, and how we'll catch up.
34. Customer profile—Sedah D'Abdul.
35. Our fourth annual *you* awards.
36. What we think is unique about us. Do you agree?
37. Communities in your neighborhood, and several on the Web.
38. Your blog posts: Javier Mendoza suggests ways we could improve.
39. Companies to consider when you get too big for us.
40. Why we believe participation pays off.
41. Meet our four favorite customer service reps for September.
42. Vendors that serve us so we can help you.
43. Our global plan—Vietnam, Italy, and your backyard.
44. What we look for in our leadership.
45. Video—our new smaller offices downtown.
46. Green is our new favorite color—save energy and money with your _____.
47. How corporate responsibility saved us $3 million last year.
48. Growing up but staying fun.
49. Your event, our treat.
50. Five promises we've kept over the past few years.

You tell me: Were there some squirmy parts in there? Can you see how customers might react to reading these? I wrote almost every one of these with the customer in mind as the reader. How would you change these if your reader were someone else in your list of stakeholders? What would you add or delete?

Growing Your Audience: Some Basics

My friend and former coworker, Mike Desjardins[156] asked me how people go about growing a blogging audience. It's a great question. I run into tons of people who have wonderful blogs,[157] blogs that deserve much more attention than they receive. What gives? What can you do to grow your audience? If you want to grow your audience, you first need to know who they are, then give them easy-to-consume chunks of content, promote your work effectively, and be persistent.

LET'S START WITH AUDIENCE

First and foremost, who are you writing this blog for? If the answer is "myself" and you have more than one RSS subscriber, congratulations. You've done it. If the answer is, "Anyone into _____," (e.g., "anyone into tech") and you have more than 10 subscribers, congratulations. Be clear about the audience.

---

[156]http://mikedesjardins.us/
[157]http://conversationagent.com/

If I'm going to bother giving you some of my time, I want something back.

Let's take Mitch Joel's Six Pixels of Separation.[158] This is a top-shelf blog, with clearly written content, that speaks to people looking to better understand the future of digital influence. Brilliant work, considerately written, and created in such a way that I come away thinking about how this impacts me. Perfect. Spot-on.

Other great examples of focused blogs that target audiences well:

- Problogger.net
- WebWorkerDaily.com
- Copyblogger.com
- 300WordsADay.com (This is a religious blog by my friend, Jon Swanson. Being that I'm not very religious, it should tell you that I love his writing and his engagement methods, no matter what he's writing about. That he makes me think about religion is a bonus.)

Technically, I could give you links all night, but the point is this. Look at how the content is focused on a specific audience. Look forward a few posts and then back. With few exceptions, you can tell exactly who the audience is.

Want to find some more decent blogs? Check out alltop .com. It's the Internet's magazine rack.

---

[158]www.twistimage.com/blog

YOUR CONTENT NEEDS TO BE WELL CHUNKED

First, journalists know this, but I'll tell you: Start with the best stuff right up at the top. Don't do it as a buildup. Second, make it such that people can read it in chunks. Check out my blog at http://chrisbrogan.com. I have headings that break up the post. I have bullets that break up the post. I've led with a graphic.

Break things up so that human eyes can read them easier. Dense posts and superlong posts are a turnoff. Oh, and that's another thing. Brevity. It rules. Pass it on.

PROMOTE YOUR BLOG EFFECTIVELY

First, make sure there's a very prominently displayed link for folks to subscribe to your RSS feed for your blog. The bigger and more attention-drawing, the better. Second, add an e-mail subscription option to your blog. I prefer using FeedBurner to manage all that. When I added a very explicit "Get this blog sent to your e-mail" button on my site, my subscriptions *leapt* up.

Second, be sure your blog's URL is loaded into pretty much every social network where you belong. Add it to MySpace, Facebook, Twitter, LinkedIn, Plaxo, Flickr, and wherever else you can bring awareness. Make sure you submit it to directories like Yahoo! and Google. Get that URL out there where people can find it. I've had lots of interesting moments where someone has found my blog via Facebook or LinkedIn.

Third, add it to your e-mail signature and your business cards. If your company doesn't give you business cards, go to

Overnight Prints,[159] Vista Print,[160] or Moo[161] and buy some. For 30 dollars or so, they help people find you (and your blog!).

In services like Twitter, promote your blog posts from time to time. Not *every* post, but ones where you feel you've done well. I never use automatic post-to-Twitter links. They just don't seem to net decent conversations. Instead, try using a conversational tone. For instance, when I'm finished posting, I will send Twitter a message something like this: "I shared my thoughts on growing your audience. What are *your* ideas?" Then I link to my post. You don't have to follow, but you'll know exactly why I asked for your attention.

One quick note: It's not always about your blog. Don't be "that person."

BE PERSISTENT

I could also say, "Be consistent," but in this case, I want you to persist in not only putting out your content, but also in making it better. *All of us* can make our stuff better. I would do well to focus on my takeaways. You might need to pare down your word count. There's *always* room to do better work.

Furthermore, try lots of new things. Stretch out the medium. Think of new ways to ask the same old questions.

[159]http://OvernightPrints.com
[160]http://VistaPrint.com
[161]http://Moo.com

Decide on challenging approaches to blogging in ways that powerfully reveal the information your audience seeks from you. Persist in such matters, never accepting that your work is flawless, but instead analyzing your responses and your increase or decrease in traffic, giving more effort accordingly.

AND NOW, THE BONUS ROUND

Another way that I've increased traffic to my blog is a basic tenet: Comment on great blogs. Write and submit guest posts to top blogs in space similar to yours (but be careful of *how* you guest-post[162]). Add occasional links to your blog posts in places like Flickr. Consider contests. Participate in other people's events. Find groups of bloggers you like and see if you fit into their circles of friends. Write a series so that people want to participate and come back for more. Make your URL memorable.

And beyond all that? Be as human as possible—in the most interesting senses of that idea. Make sense?

---

[162]www.problogger.net/archives/2008/06/06/when-guest-posts-become-too-self-centered/

Be Effective in Meetings, and Use Social Media Tools

Joshua Cohen asked me to discuss how I go about running meetings effectively. Josh and his business partner, Jamison Tilsner, run Tilzy.TV,[163] an Internet TV start-up. I knew right away that I could give some effectiveness advice that would include examples of using social media and Internet tools effectively at the same time.

THREE TYPES OF MEETINGS

First, realize that for most businesses, there are essentially three types of meetings:

1. Announcement meeting
2. Status meeting
3. Brainstorm meeting

These are ranked in order of how fast they should run and/ or how interactive they should be.

---

[163]http://Tilzy.TV

ANNOUNCEMENT MEETING

An *announcement* meeting, which should be superfast, is reserved for announcements that you want to make in person to your team. You might use this to announce funding, to announce the addition of a new key employee (and, at a start-up, *every* employee is key), or to announce a major shift in direction. It should have one speaker (two, max), and doesn't require much in the way of social media, except that you might consider videotaping the announcement (either for future use in documenting the company's experiences or as potential YouTube press release material).

STATUS MEETING

A *status* meeting, which should be reasonably quick, is a chance for all teams to be heard from. However, it's not for discussion. Instead, the project manager calling the meeting (and, at a start-up, lots of people get to play project manager) should have gone around ahead of the meeting to get the status. Get all the conversation out of people by hearing them fully *outside* the meeting.

Then, at the meeting, the person who gathered status reports merely announces that he or she will be running down the current status. That person gives a very brief status message, naming the applicable person or department, and moves on to the next person. It's not a time for discussion. If someone wants to open a discussion, the moderator should interrupt as politely but as quickly as possible and offer to meet on an individual basis after the meeting, but the first and foremost part of the meeting is to run down a status.

Social media and Internet tools that are useful in meetings include wikis, for simple note taking, or perhaps an internal blog might be the better for that job. (What do *you* think?) You might use a tool like Utterli to record the status meeting, and team members can listen to the status directly after the fact.

BRAINSTORMING MEETING

A *brainstorming* meeting is probably the most open-ended and least simple to run. In these meetings, you're asking people to discuss open-ended futures. This should be clearly announced at the beginning of the meeting (as well as in the invitation) so that people know it's going to be a conversation and not a quick in-and-out meeting.

Some things to make a meeting like this run better: Lay out the goals and end points so that people know what they're aiming toward. When discussions become too tangential, help people back toward the goals and end points. Another tip: Have one person outside the brainstorming flow keep an eye on the time, and also a notion of the goals, so that he or she can guide people back onto the targets at hand.

One social media tool that is useful at brainstorming sessions is the mind-mapping tool MindMeister,[164] which captures free-form ideas in a visual way that can be shared later by a variety

---

[164]www.MindMeister.com

of methods. Another tool you could use for brainstorming: a shared tumbleblog on Tumblr, where people can clip in various bits of information to share their vision of a project. Need visuals? Don't forget Flickr for finding photos to use internally for the discussion (be mindful of their Creative Commons status).

TIPS FOR *ALL* MEETINGS

The purpose of meetings is to involve more than one person in informational alignment. In some cases, that means asking for information. In lots of cases, it means doling out status. Here are some tips for every type of meeting you hold:

- Brevity is your friend. Meetings longer than one-half hour are evil.
- Start on time. Finish on time. Meetings that wait for late people encourage lateness at subsequent meetings.
- The boss isn't the boss of the meeting. If it's your meeting, be polite, but be firm.
- Copious notes aren't a virtue. Understanding next actions are a virtue.
- Every idea needs an owner. If you come up with what has to come next, the *next* thing you do is find out who owns it, and when, roughly, that person will accomplish the task.
- Some meetings are just well-worded e-mail messages and an updated project plan, meaning that *no* meeting is necessary. Trim where you can. People loathe meetings, and the people who love them usually have something wrong with them.

Programming for the Masses: Social Computing

You are learning how to program information using new languages that have yet to be written. You might not be building the next spreadsheet software or the next Internet browser, but I think that what you're building might have more impact than previous software. As we learn to navigate social networks and make media, I believe we are crafting a language that will execute complex requests, deliver information back and forth between vast and distributed databases, and overlay the way business is being done in the future.

SEEDS FOR THE CONVERSATION

I spend time in bookstores. Sometimes, I compile lists of books I want to read. Other times, I read portions or complete selections of books.

In early 2008, I read *The Big Switch*, Nicholas Carr's book describing how companies like Amazon and Google have paved the way for "utility computing." The basic premise is that electricity in the 1900s went from being generated on-site to being generated centrally, and that businesses stopped having to understand power generation and could thus focus on their business. Carr says companies like Amazon, with their S3 storage and their EC2 computers, and Google with search, Docs, and other apps, are letting us focus on programs instead of the gear. That's the first seed.

Mixed into my thinking as well are a couple of essays out of *Hackers and Painters,* by Paul Graham (which talks about big ideas from the computing age), and *Everything Is Miscellaneous,* by David Weinberger, about how we're learning to sort and organize information by different methods than we did in previous centuries.

Graham has an essay explaining programming languages, and especially how most programming languages people are learning these days are far abstracted from what computers need to know to do what they do. That's one seed. I started realizing that the things we're learning to do in social networks, in making social media like blogs, podcasts, wikis, and in video, are in essence, programming languages.

Weinberger's book is some of the glue needed for the theory. His ideas, which involve the notion of how information is stored and retrieved, relate to my view of our new "databases."

WHAT ARE WE LEARNING

If you think about it, we're learning bits of programming for this new social computing every day. If you understand how to use Twitter, with the @s and the direct messages, and the flow of conversation, you know a rudimentary "language." In Facebook, you understand how to read and interpret the news stream, and you know where to seek data to synthesize information. As you learn how to blog, how to link, how to embed other technologies, you learn how to build user interfaces, how to structure queries, and how to generate reports.

WHAT WE CAN DO

So far, we're learning only the basics. Hey, we're *writing* the language, yet we are using our social computing language for our own projects. For instance, the Frozen Pea Fund[165] was a project built by threading several social networks together to build a system to help fund a breast cancer funding setup. In other cases, we're building conversations in Utterli that might be informal today but that build themselves into different structures as we learn how to use them.

Most people see social computing as a tool for marketing and PR, but these are just the first rudimentary applications. We can do much more with our skills on social networks, and our ability to make, consume, distribute, and interact with social media.

WHERE CAN WE TAKE THIS

If we learn how to program in these new languages, and if we understand how to use these new forms of databases, we can

---

[165]http://frozenpeafund.com/

learn how to use this type of programming for our business and organizational needs. Watch someone who's adept at searching eBay[166] and Craigslist go after what they're looking to purchase. Observe someone who knows how to use LinkedIn for more than just surfing business histories.

We are out there, learning. And this isn't propeller head stuff. This is understanding real information for real application in the real world. Your understanding of these new social computing systems is heading us into an interesting new phase, soon to be as commonplace as understanding how to use the card swipe at the grocery store

Can you see it? Are you with me? Or is this too far a stretch?

36

Creatives and Your Secret Mission

For every day we don't unlock our own value, we remain plugged into our other identity. I twittered this sentiment, but I believe it applies to a lot of *you*. You have ideas and thoughts and realizations

---

[166]www.eBay.com

that rise above what you're called upon to accomplish in a given day.

You can choose a few paths: One is to just do what you're given to do, go home, and wonder why life hasn't dropped off a big fat bag of cash and destiny on your doorstep. Another is to fight the system at every turn and to rail against everyone that they don't "get it" and that you're smarter than all of them, no matter how it looks right now.

Or you can work on your secret mission. Realize that you're different. Cloak some of that during your day-job hours by doing more than is necessary without drawing much attention to the fact that you're doing it. If your workplace is ripe for change from within, be that agent quietly. If not, then work on what you will do outside of what you're paid to do to build on that secret mission.

The point is, there's what you *take* to be reality, and then there's what you *make* to be reality. The more you work on the latter, even if it's your secret mission, the more you can grow your abilities, find ways to satisfy what you know is true, and move into bigger things.

Or you can complain about how "everyone else doesn't get it."

To prove you're not crazy, I recommend reading Richard Florida's *Rise of the Creative Class: And How It's Transforming Work, Leisure, Community and Everyday Life.*

Advice for Traditional and Local News Media

Someone, a brave someone, from Boston's local TV news scene submitted a question to a panel with representatives from MySpace, Facebook, Eons, IBM, and a virtual worlds builder. She said she wanted to know the role of traditional media in this space, and what road she and her organization should get on for the future of media. Panel members' answers were all over the map, but Jeff Taylor (founder of Monster and Eons) had the start of a thoughtful answer, and his response blended with something someone else said earlier (either Jeff again or perhaps Tom Arrix of Facebook): that if we observe the Super Bowl ads for 2008, we'll notice that the majority of them point us to a Web property. With this as backdrop, here's some advice.

BE BRIEF ON AIR, GO DEEPER OFF AIR

The current champion of this method is NPR[167], which posts all its on-air materials, including longer versions of interviews,

---

[167]http://NPR.org

on its web site for further review. For people you want to know about, watching or listening to just the snippets that make the news isn't always enough. Having the option to go deeper is a great service that takes advantage of all the quality work a journalistic team has put into the experience.

This provides added value for people interested in a particular story, but it's also clever for marketing and understanding your customer base. We track and observe and understand the behaviors of people so that we may better serve them. That's the first-line value.

INTEGRATE LOCAL SOCIAL MEDIA TYPES

Papers and TV are still missing an opportunity to draft independent media makers into their work. They should move to an upstream editorial and curation relationship with people who can go into their own communities, reveal stories of interest to those communities, and then bring this body of work to editors and curators who can understand which of these stories are right for the air, which would do fine on the Web, and which might merit further professional reporting, with a hat tip to the original creator.

EMBED COMMUNITY TECHNOLOGY INTO YOUR SITES

Pluck up the best blogs and video blogs in the area. Build community conversation sections, even if that invites critics to come out and shoot at your stories a bit. Gannett did this really well with MomsLikeMe.[168] Build chat rooms for during-the-news discussion experiences. There are tons of ways to empower the voice of your audience to have reciprocal value. These are just a few. You probably have a few more.

MAKE YOUR MEDIA PORTABLE

Take some of the deep stories and make podcasts out of them. Give us embedded codes for your media. Make a spot for metadata like user tagging. Give us ways to build your media into our sites and spread your word to more sources.

SWITCH SENSATION FOR CAUSES AND EMPOWERMENT

We put a premium on stories of what's going wrong in the world. Of course, it's important to know about some of the bad news that's happening out there, but why doesn't the *local* news offer stories about where we can help? Why aren't we learning about people doing great work more often? Right now, such stories have a slot at the very end of the newscast, where the two or three people behind the desk make that weird half smile.

Push up the empowerment stories, and bring that into your deep Web coverage as well.

---

[168]http://MomsLikeMe.com

RANDOM IDEAS

One more thing: Do we *need* everyone at a desk with monitors behind them, or sitting in fake living rooms? Aren't there other settings? We haven't mixed it up much for more than 50 years. I guess this isn't social media advice—but hey.

Social Networks Are Your Local Pubs

Walking out the door the other night to watch the Super Bowl last year was interesting. I walked past the Barking Dog (a local bar), past the Ale House (another bar), past the Carriage Wheel, and then into the Stage 2 Cinema Pub, which is normally a movie theater, but when there's a big sports event, it transforms into a great place to watch a game. I realized that any one of those places I walked past had people watching the game. I knew that each one of those places had "regulars" and "visitors" and a sense of what's okay and what draws disapproving stares. Sounds a bit like social networks, if you squint.

WHAT HAPPENS AT PUBS

Laura "Pistachio" Fitton called Twitter a village.[169] That's one way to look at it, as lots of different things happen there, and her analogy works out well. I'm going to go another way. I'm going to compare Twitter to what happens at a pub. And I'm going to compare Utterli and Facebook and Seesmic and Yahoo! Groups and Digg to all kinds of other pubs. Jonathan Schwartz blogged recently[170] about Sun's intent to reinvigorate its software communities. Another pub.

Pubs are where people talk. There's news. There's gossip. There are deals and selling. There are pronouncements. There are silly moments. There are conversations and chance, random happenings. The thing is, pubs aren't places where you do things. They are places where you talk about things. Right? They might be where the seeds of ideas come from (lots of the work of the Founding Fathers of the United States germinated in pubs), but the actual work and doing took place elsewhere.

ARE PUBS NECESSARY?

Yes! Pub is short for *public house,* and there is evidence of pubs serving as a valuable incubator in the history of several nations. They are places where people of all backgrounds can gather, although, as is true of most social situations, some feel left out

---

[169]http://pistachioconsulting.com

[170]http://blogs.sun.com/jonathan/entry/communities_then_customers_forrester_on

or unwelcome at certain pubs. In general, pubs serve as common ground where people can come to be refreshed, to talk, to meet with both like-minded and dissenting people.

IF SOCIAL NETWORKS ARE PUBS

First, be ready to buy someone else a drink. Take that as a metaphor for sharing overall. If you're a marketer, share something of value to me. If you're an aspiring blogger, ask to hear my story first. If you're a salesperson, do something for me before launching into what's in it for you.

Second, mind the place. Pubs aren't run by the barkeep. They're run by the people who come there often enough to set the place straight, who know when a stranger might need welcoming, and who will keep an eye on the place while you're taking care of something in the back. This means a two-way relationship between the barkeep/management and the regulars. How you manage that makes all the difference in the world.

Finally, if you look through that lens and consider these networks as pubs and the other people there as pubgoers, one thing comes right to mind: It's not what you do *inside* the pub that makes you or changes you or gives you something to call your own; it's what you do *outside* the pub that counts in the long run.

With this in mind, let's talk about pubs. Where do you go for your drinks? Where is the conversation good? What discourse, new ideas, and challenges are you getting out of this pub of yours that you can then work on outside the pub? Or is my idea all suds and no beer?

Facebook and the Social Graph: Who Benefits

Sometimes it takes a while for something to sink in. Facebook asks me for all kinds of information on how I know the people I accept as friends, but I realized that I get nothing out of the exchange and that Facebook and potential advertisers gain tons.

Populating the social graph for Facebook is essentially modeling even more data for advertisers to absorb into their information banks. This isn't 100 percent bad. For instance, if advertisers looked at every friend I had and noticed that only 11 of them *ever* clicked a Facebook ad, wouldn't that tell them something? If my friends and their friends (by extension) all seem to spend time very actively on Facebook apps, that might reveal the value of building an application versus buying a more passive ad.

And who owns that data? For instance, suppose a "friend" on her own page links to me, and now we're linked as "friends" in Facebook. I can see her data, read her updates, and so on. But can I extrapolate that data out of the environment? I would hope not. Because it's one thing if we're real friends, but what if she's someone who maliciously just wants to slurp my data, add it to some kind of spammy marketing project, and move on?

I ask *you*: Who benefits from Facebook's Social Graph data? Just a thought worth considering while building your social media plans.

The Value of Networks

You purchase a plane ticket and fly to a new city for the first time. You take a cab to the heart of the city and then realize you're hungry for a bite to eat. You open your laptop and steal wifi, trying to find a restaurant, and realize you've left your laptop power cord at home and will need to find a replacement. You get a call on your cell from your aunt saying that she needs to buy a new digital camera and asks which one should she get, because she's standing in Best Buy right now. You see a new e-mail come in from your boss stating that you're fired.

YOUR NETWORK: THE OLD DAYS

In a bygone era, your network was your family, your neighbors, your coworkers, and a few scattered others. You lived reasonably close to some number of these people, and they knew your comings and goings as intimately as a Facebook news stream. These people knew you when you were a foolish kid, and they knew that you weren't very good at math, but that you were a hard worker. If you needed help with something, you could reach out by mail, by phone, by asking around. It took a while, but usually someone could find something.

YOUR NETWORK: THE NEW DAYS

Several of your "friends" aren't that. They're more like "friend-lies." They agree to be part of your network. You can reach more people than ever before. They're all over the world. They have different roles, different networks of their own. The combined sum of what these people know in the aggregate is exponential. They might not know you the way a cousin or a junior high school teacher would know you, but they are willing to do some level of information sharing with you.

WHAT DO I MEAN BY *NETWORK?*

The concept of a network means a connection of things that form something larger in sum. Networked computers mean that you can access some resources back and forth and communicate. Social networks (in the software sense) mean that the software makes a connectivity between users. Networks in the human sense mean that we have chosen to align ourselves in some form or fashion around common beliefs, goals, values, or something similar.

Organized religion works on the power of networks. So do labor unions. So do governments. Business is ultimately about networks of one kind or another.

WHAT CAN A NETWORK DO?

Networks are about sharing resources. It's the same for computers, social networks, human networks, and pretty much all kinds. Thus, if you're looking to build a good network of people, sharing has to be the common link. Networks can help someone raise money quickly. They can direct lots of attention toward the same point. They can help people find jobs. They can elect government officials. They can shift power and resources seamlessly.

NOT A NUMBERS GAME ... OR IS IT?

I think some of the value of a network comes from its numbers.

In social networks, I'm fortunate to have a reasonably good number of "friends." Partly, it's because I've been fortunate enough to attend a lot of conferences, and I've been diligent about meeting lots of people. Partly, it's because I publish a blog. Partly, it's because I do a lot of work to link things together, to *form* networks by inviting people to certain social networks, to accept requests from people, to build out the digital structure of such things.

Here are some quick tidbits:

- I'm not in any way a "collector" of friends in social networks. At this point, I say yes to most anyone trying to connect, but I don't gather.

- I don't believe in the "rule" that you must "really in real life" know someone before accepting that person as a "friend."

- I don't build networks to market. I'm not a marketer. I build networks to be helpful and to deliver value in both directions.

- I think the key to it all is this: "More hands lighten the load."

TIPS ON BUILDING VALUABLE NETWORKS

Here's my quick definition of *value*: I don't mean money. I mean the ability to deliver and receive information, to help, and to further development (of networks, information, capabilities).

I can only tell you what I believe has worked best for me. I imagine your mileage may vary. I hope others add their own ideas about building networks in the comments section at http://chrisbrogan.com/comments-from-101.

- Be friendly and inclusive. When I go to conferences, I look for the fringe players, the people who aren't well known but who are interesting. Sometimes, these turn into amazingly wonderful connections.

- Treat "big names" like real people, and oddly, they'll treat *you* like a real person. This comes in handy later, when you can be helpful.

- Seek to be helpful. Always. The more you can do for others, the more that wheel comes around, should you find yourself in need.

- Connect. Connect. Connect. Help others find each other. Connect people with other people as often as humanly possible. This keeps the flow moving, and it shows that you're into sharing.

- *Beware of network leeches.* Occasionally, in trying to form communities of useful and sharing people, someone comes along who needs, needs, needs. Learn how to cut that sort away from your network. It's not rude. It's not elitist.

- Diversity and opportunity are great ways to build something more interesting. Homogenous networks are only useful in a narrow scope, meaning that you should strive to meet lots of good people from lots of walks of life. You never know.

- Say thank you. Often.

- Do as much as you can, and then offer to help connect others to even more help, if you can.

- Be as timely as possible. Help isn't much help if it's too late.

- Never take credit. Always assume responsibility. Be as humble as you can muster.

- Give often and long before you ever have to ask for something for you.

SOCIAL NETWORKS AND *YOUR* NETWORK OF VALUE

The power of all these social software applications is that they empower us to communicate rapidly, in a one-to-many format, and along the lines of our networks of value. To that end, be sure to use this to accomplish your goals. Make sure you know the size and depth of your personal database. Make sure your contacts and connections are well connected through these digital tools. Try to build them all such that you can respond quickly to people's needs, that you can reach the edges of your network and help others extend out to theirs, so that everyone may enjoy the full effect of that work.

Don't be evil. (Easy, right?)

I consider your participation a value of my network. The fact that you come and share your ideas and insights is wonderful to me. I'm not always near a computer to respond to every comment, but I read everything you say, and I *love* it when someone in the comments section of my blog communicates to someone else, and when my readers go off and blog their own take on the original idea that takes it in another direction. Thank you for this. I'm forever grateful.

41

Five Things to Do at a Social Networking Meetup

Meetups (and, more recently, "tweetups," which are meetups organized via Twitter) are the online manifestation of our social networking efforts. With Twitter and Upcoming.org[171] and Facebook and all the other social networks, putting together a bunch of like-minded people is relatively simple. You find a venue that doesn't mind a bunch of nerds, preferably with a place you can be loud (because social media types are often the loudest bunch in there, unless there's a bachelorette party), and, hopefully, some delightful libations to ease social interaction. But what do you *do* there, once you've walked in and identified that you're in the right place? Here's a recipe.

SAY HI TO YOUR KNOWN FRIENDS

Oftentimes, someone at the meetup is known to you. Make sure you say hi to that person earlier in the night rather than later. I'm working on this one, because sometimes, I'll be somewhere with friends and never get over to see them because time gets eaten up

---

[171]http://upcoming.yahoo.com

so fast. I'm going to make a point of saying hi to my longer-known friends first at meetups, so that they'll feel acknowledged.

FIND THE NEW PEOPLE

Look for folks who might be new to your local scene, or those you haven't met before, and introduce yourself. My favorite opening line is to ask them what they normally do when they're not hanging out with a bunch of Twitter geeks. If that doesn't work, I like to ask people about their passions.

DON'T CROWD-SURF TOO MUCH

There's a tendency that's easy to follow to just flit among the crowd. It's not a wedding. You don't have to hit every table. If you find something interesting, don't be afraid to dive deep into the conversation for a bit. Get into some deeper waters with people, because otherwise, time will wash over you like a wave and you'll be out without much to show for it.

IF YOU NEED TO DO BUSINESS

Try to think of these meetups as a first date. Don't put your tongue down our throats. In other words, if you're there fishing for new business, play it cool and be part of the gang. Talk about what's relevant, and don't swerve instantly into your line of business and how you can help (sell) us. However, it's okay to say that you're hoping to build business relationships or the like. Just save the details for a follow-up conversation.

TALK ABOUT SOMETHING NEW

Whenever possible, bring along some really neat new idea to throw into the mix. Think of it as mental show-and-tell. Or, if you have a nifty new something to show people, do real-world show-and-tell. Bringing something new to the meetup will enrich everything. (Don't force it into the conversation, but have something new in mind.)

42

Delivering Content Value to Market Your Product

BatchBlue knows how to reach out and deliver value up front. I'll admit that I had no idea what BatchBlue[172] was before early 2008. There are too many great companies out there, and I don't know them *all*! So, how cool is it that Michelle Riggen-Ransom reaches out to me, citing applicable posts I've written over the past few months, then offers me a really informative "blue paper" on social media? (It's like a white paper—only blue.)

---

[172]http://batchblue.com/

This turns out to be a great way to deliver value. Brian Clark of Copyblogger has made this his model all along. Deliver great content and value, and then make your offer on the other side of it. In this case, Michelle and Adam Darowski and the team have software to sell for contact, task, and communications management. But they lead by giving us a useful paper to consider. For some, there's not a lot *new* in the document, but it's a good resource, well formatted, and looks shiny and useful.

The old way of marketing was to put up a "free white paper" and hope that people would give you their e-mail address so that you could market them into submission. The new way is to create useful information or tools and share them for free with your community, without attempting lead capture, then hope that this goodwill translates into links (which help you with search) and also potential prospects.

For more on this mind-set, see the book *Inbound Marketing*, by Brian Halligan and Dharmesh Shah.

43

The Community Play

Publishers are scratching at this right now: How do we turn our publications into communities? In the magazine world,

FastCompany[173] augmented its magazine site with a social network. Last year's Gnomedex[174] conference used introNetworks[175] to power people-to-people connectivity before the event started. Webkinz[176] knows it's not about the cloth or the stuffing. But these are just the start. There are so many obvious community business opportunities in play, just waiting to happen. Why?

Here are some options for some community organizations not yet in play.

HOTEL SOCIAL NETWORKS

Forget loyalty programs and sky miles. Imagine a program where business types can opt in to reveal that they're staying at a particular hotel and that they're amenable to meetings about product pitches, but not job offers, for the next four days. The upside? I'd pay *extra* to go where the business opportunities would make it worthwhile.

Fear Factor: Stalkers and other liabilities. This can't be too hard to solve, can it?

HARRY POTTER

Marketers have merchandised the life out of the books, everything from pretend wands to real jelly beans, and there's a massively

---

[173]http://FastCompany.com

[174]http://Gnomedex.com

[175]http://introNetworks.com

[176]www.Webkinz.com

multiplayer videogame in the works (or has it launched?), but what's missing is a place where fans of the books and movies can get together, talk about them, create their own fan fictions and mash-ups, and otherwise sit there in a barrel to be hit with opportunities that would work best for them.

Fear Factor: Kids in the mix means different privacy laws, so, again, stalkers/predators are part of it.

THE NFL (OR YOUR SPORTS INDUSTRY HERE)

During the 2008 Super Bowl, I was at a local cinema pub watching my team melt down on a 40-foot-wide screen in a roomful of people. I'm a casual attendee, but sports fans are passionate. Where there's passion, there's an opportunity for a community play in social networking. Why not have some kind of site to share videos, pictures, audio, and more? It's obvious that there would be a difference in quality between what an NFL fan would produce and what a huge organization dedicated to the best-crafted sports media can whip up. Allow for profiles, for chats, and maybe even for on-NFL-site fantasy football, an opportunity you want anyway yet haven't figured out how to approach.

Fear Factor: My best guess here is copyright and other legal stuff.

TRADE OR NONPROFIT ASSOCIATIONS

Most trade association web sites are brochureware from the 1990s. They have a home page, an About page, a contact page, a calendar, and maybe one more wild-card page. Here are situations where you have hundreds and/or thousands of members and prospective members who might find value in connecting to each other, as well as to you. Make it easier. Build a space for side-by-side connecting, as well as the part of your site just giving out information.

Fear Factor: I don't think there is a fear factor, unless it's just fear of cost to upgrade their sites.

ANYWHERE YOU HAVE A POPULATION OF LIKE-MINDED PEOPLE

There are community plays inherent in most every situation where you have tons and tons of motivated customers waiting to be converted into even more valuable community members. I could keep naming them, but the preceding examples should get your head moving. In all cases, I provided a fear factor that might keep people from executing. You may or may not agree with me that these are the reasons why people *wouldn't* execute a community play. But if you disagree, you'll have to share what else might be holding them down.

Whatever the case, I think there are opportunities not yet being explored. What do *you* think?

44

The Power of Links

A while back, I read a blog post by Kevin Burton about how Google had implemented "nofollow" on all posted links as a baseline behavior on its new Sites implementation. (Briefly, this means that when Google's or anyone else's spiders go out and see what's on a web site, they don't follow links to other sites to see what those sites are and index them as well.) Now, I'm not a search guy, so I'm not sure what Google's reasons are for this. But here's what this has me thinking about.

LINKS SIGNIFY INTENTION

This relates to what Steve Gillmor talks about with regard to gestures[177] and attention and the like. If I put a link in a blog post, it suggests that I find value in what lies at the other end of the link. It means that I think *you* should click the link and see what's going on.

So think about that for a moment. Think about *your* behavior with links. When you write about Britt Raybould's Bold Words blog,[178] but you *don't* put a link to it, you're signifying that you're not interested in people following the link to discover her work.

---

[177]http://gesturelab.com/

[178]www.bold-words.com/

When you talk about LinkedIn, but you link it back to your own blog post instead of to LinkedIn, you're signifying that you want to keep traffic on your site. *Sometimes* this makes sense. If I said, "Here's my other article about LinkedIn," then that makes sense. But if *every* link keeps the audience on your site, you're telling me that you don't want me wandering around the Web sharing attention.

LINKS BUILD NETWORKS OF THOUGHT

Years ago, when I got the first-ever Mac, it came with HyperCard. It was *so* amazing to me. I could link up words inside of text and give you all kinds of nuance and reference and sidebar conversations, all the while keeping the original document in-line. Links are part of that same magic, only better. Because HyperCard, at least when I was starting out with it, was relegated to referencing my own computer and documents, whereas links let me point all over the Web.

To that end, you can build amazing and interesting networks of thought. You can build posts that give people an understanding about something by synthesizing data *for* them. Sometimes, you're not the authority, but you are always in a position to thread up some articles, videos, and other resources to build out something of use to you. Being helpful means finding the right resources for the point you're hoping to make.

LINKS GIVE CREDIT

If you click the photo included in a blog post, it takes you back to the artist who created it. Though it's not a perfect way to give credit (Steve Garfield[179] schools me on this all the time), it's better than just using the picture in my blog post—and better than just writing, "Jared did this work."

In this world of free, one of the *only* currencies we still seek and demand are links. Note that my work is all available to you for free, to repurpose in lots of ways. The only thing you can't legally do with my work is directly make money from it. (Mind you, if my ideas help you make money because you *execute* them in your own way, you get to keep that with my blessings.) However, you can repost every single blog post I put out on your blog, on your dog's blog, wherever you want, *provided* you give a link back to me at www.chrisbrogan.com. That's not asking a lot in return for all that I put into my work. Right?

So, links are a very important piece of Internet currency. They are the currency of *attention* in that way.

LINKS *ARE* THE NETWORK

Your phone has plenty of buttons on it, but until you push them in the right order, it's a lot of capacity and not enough intent. Building web pages like blogs and wikis and the like are *your* chance to build a network of your own intentions. We do this all the time. FriendFeed is a tool to show you links to my entire Web presence. So is Lijit.[180] Twitter, blogs, and everywhere that we can input HTML are ways to thread the needle.

179http://stevegarfield.com/
180http://Lijit.com

When you add links to a page, you tell a story. You build networks of value. For example, if you build a blog post called "The Top 20 Torrent Sites," you've just given others a resource to improve their Web experience.

Go forth. Create networks. Learn how to make nice, beautiful, useful links, give people credit and signal your intentions, and thread a beautiful net for people who can use your help.

The return value is how this all ends up working for us. Doc Searls[181] might call this a way to make money "because of value" from what we're doing. ("Because of" effect is making money because of something rather than with it.) Do you agree?

Authority, Ownership, and Mechanics

Three things change the way we're using these tools for social media: authority, ownership, and mechanics. These are three of

---

[181]http://blogs.law.harvard.edu/doc/2008/02/29/some-views-on-the-blogosystem/

the five sources of a revolution, as stated by Moshe Yudkowsky in a podcast I heard recently. Here are my definitions for these three terms. *Authority*: "Who has the ability to change things?" *Ownership*: "Who owns what we create?" *Mechanics*: "How do we put it all together?" If you look at what matters to us in this age of making social media, using the Web our way, and sharing information, I believe these are the three forces in play.

Now the question becomes: How do you, as a professional, as a business, as someone with a product or service, contemplate those forces on *your* ideas, products, services, deliverables? Are *you* the sole author of your efforts? Do *you* own the intellectual property, or have you open-sourced it? Who can tinker with how it is used, displayed, and/or consumed?

It's easy to think about these things when we're talking about someone else: "Record industry: Let music be free," but does it become a bit more difficult when you consider *you* and *your* relationship to these ideas?

Authority, ownership, mechanics. How do these forces impact what you're doing?

46

Enabling Peer Collaboration Using Social Networks

A friend from the United Kingdom writes to ask me how she might help her somewhat traditional trade association see the value of using a social networking application to facilitate communications between association members, and maybe also as a way to encourage new members to participate. Trade associations are a perfect type of organization to employ social networking tools to encourage conversations and build digital relationships. Here are some potential next steps.

KEEP THE TECHNOLOGY PART SIMPLE

In situations where people aren't exactly techies, keep the energy on the benefits of collaboration and cross-team communication. To that end, I recommend a simple but functional platform like Ning, or if it has to be managed inside the firewall, maybe something like JiveSoftware[182] or Mzinga.[183]

---

[182] www.jivesoftware.com

[183] http://Mzinga.com

BUILD IT OUT A BIT

Starting with a big empty platform is scary. I recommend building out a few user accounts for some members, and maybe finding a few "friendlies" to build a profile and start messaging back and forth. It always feels easier to understand when you can see real-world examples of members using the system. Round up about a half-dozen people who might be more inclined to "get it," help them build an account, add a user pic, and so on, and then send a few messages back and forth. Then, when you display and/or demonstrate to the member base, they will see themselves in it.

MAKE A SCREENCAST

Use a software like Jing[184] to shoot a quick screencast of the features and functionality. Keep it to under two minutes. The point of this is, "It's easier to see how it works than read about it."

ASSIST WITH SIGN-UPS AND 10-MINUTE TRAININGS

Tool adoption for non-tech-happy groups comes down to comfort levels. One way to counter this is to assist by taking a few days to help members sign up, even if you do this remotely via e-mail and phone. Once they're signed up, consider step-by-step training. Even making a document with 100 screen captures, pointing out which buttons to click in which order, and distributing it widely would be a step in the right direction.

---

[184]http://JingProject.com

DRIVE SOME MARKETING ATTENTION TOWARD THE NEW PLATFORM

Finally, start making it part of the organizational process. In a newsletter, instead of referring to an e-mail address for questions about a new program, invite people to post questions to the new forums in the new social network. Add a prominent link on the main web site. Add the new social network to e-mail signature files. Send out a little insert in the next paper mail drive. The point is, let people know it's there and encourage them to use it.

IT'S ABOUT THE PEOPLE

The secret about technology is that it's always about the people. When I speak with groups about how their social network isn't quite taking off in the organization, I'm often told about all the features, but never about how it was integrated into the flow of a given employee's day. That's the key.

47

10 Ways to Make Your Next Conference Better

Before your next conference, consider these 10 simple things:

1. Scour the Web (Technorati and Google Blogsearch and Twitter Search) to see who's coming, and reach out to people you want to see.

2. Schedule meetings with people on day one, as soon as you can, because time runs out.

3. Drink more water than you normally do, and wear *very* comfortable shoes.

4. Pack business cards. Tons of them. But get business cards from others, too, because then *you* can ensure a reply.

5. Have a really simple, brief answer to these questions: "What do you do?" "What are you working on these days?" "What brings you to the conference?"

6. Blog a *very recent* photo of yourself so that people know who they're going to meet.

7. Check Upcoming.org and Facebook for related events and parties. Attend a few.

8. Take some pictures of you and some folks you meet. Post them with links to the people, if you can find such.

9. Never assume people are better than you or that you're somehow not good enough or important enough. You are. And if people don't know you yet, go in as if they know you reasonably well anyway.

10. Don't hide behind your laptop, BlackBerry, camera. Step out and be brave a few times. It *will* pay off.

48

Who Is Secretly Pitching You?

Kare Anderson of Say it Better[185] pointed out this piece of fiction to me from *The New Yorker* magazine: "Raj, Bohemian"[186] is about a guy getting the distinct feeling that everyone around him has fallen into an endless cycle of promoting things. It gets to be a little much when he realizes that some of the people in his circle do this for a living, as a way of spreading the word about their clients' products and services. It's word-of-mouth marketing gone stealth. It makes me wonder about our online communities and the notion of reputation—so much so that Julien Smith and I wrote a book, *Trust Agents,* about this very thing. Here are some thoughts from a year or so before we wrote the book, to give you a sense of how we seeded those ideas.

The Internet is perfect for this kind of thing. We don't even have to see our face-to-face friends. Our new social network friends can tell us plenty about products without telling us whether they're being paid to talk about them. Should we be critical? Should we see advertisers under every stone?

---

[185] http://KareAndersonofSayitBetter.com
[186] www.newyorker.com/fiction/features/2008/03/10/080310fi_fiction_kunzru?currentPage=1

STEALTH PITCHING
AND COMMUNITIES

People are more wired than ever before. It's really easy to find holes in information, simple to fact-check a little bit. To that end, companies that are willing to risk their community's trust by pitching in a stealthy way are taking chances with their brand. Every time we see a "Wal-Marting Across America" blog,[187] it sticks with us. Sometimes, we change our behavior as consumers because of it. Other times, we don't.

By the way, I'm sure these tactics work, so let's not discount the fact that stealth pitching brings in cold, hard cash for companies.

APATHY NATION

I should point out that apathy is in abundance on such matters—and has been since the end of the 1960s (at least in America). We learned how *not* to trust our government. We understood that companies were (are) in it for the money. And in lots of cases, we shrug and we don't care. Not all of us, surely, but there are plenty of people who shrug off the things big companies do and just accept them as the status quo.

So, here we are with a lot of questions, and not many answers. We are awash in opportunities to be covertly influenced on our social networks of choice.

---

[187]www.blogher.com/node/11579

IT COMES BACK TO TRUST

I have a very healthy respect for staying true to this community. I never want you to wonder whether something I'm raving about is because someone paid me to say it. It's just not on the table. When I feel there's an external influence to something I'm saying (e.g., if I talk about Utterli, I always try to mention that I'm on the advisory board), then I will do my very best to separate that from random ravings about something. The currency of my relationship with you is trust. You won't bother reading what I have to say if you wonder about my ulterior motives.

Am I completely unbiased? No. Is anyone?

REPUTATION ENGINES

Mechanisms for trust need to find their way into social networks. Reputation systems, not unlike the ones created on eBay, LinkedIn, and Amazon,[188] would help add much-needed context and history and transparency to the "me" that floats around on the Web, on Twitter, on Facebook. Perhaps this is an opt-in situation, like logging in via OpenID, or maybe it's just some kind of third-party validation system you can send someone to, should a conversation veer into waters where it's necessary.

I'm not suggesting that privacy be surrendered. This isn't something that requires people to give up the option of having an anonymous persona on the Web. Instead, I'm saying that for people who seek to represent themselves as who they are,

---

[188]www.Amazon.com

a reputation engine might be one way to clear up some of the fears of blind stealth pitching.

DOING AN HONEST JOB

I believe that advertising and marketing and public relations can be done honestly and that turning pitches into conversations isn't inherently evil. I believe people *do* want to understand products and services and have a relationship with certain brands. My concern is with tactics, and especially with how people might use social networks and social media to forward an agenda without being explicit about their involvement.

I never want to discount the good work that professional advertising, marketing, and PR people are doing with social networks.

ARE YOU SECRETLY BEING PITCHED?

Some would argue that we're *all* pitching something. When I use Twitter to share the link to this post, that's a pitch. When I show you my nifty new e-book, that's a pitch. But the question is more about the hidden motives than about whether you're being encouraged in one direction or another.

49

The Sound of Content Ripping Free from Its Page

Yahoo's announcement in March 2008 that it intends to introduce a different method of search—such that Yahoo! will pull microformatted data out of a page and deliver it on Yahoo's results instead of passing the searcher through to the target page—should send a shiver through the minds of SEO experts and content producers alike. Let me explain it again: Imagine search results that don't encourage users to land on your web site but instead serve them answers at the search results page. Sweating yet?

From a user's perspective, this is much more useful in certain situations. In the Blogspotting article,[189] Stephen Baker uses the example of someone looking for restaurant info. Instead of getting links to all kinds of pages where the info is housed, you'll get a simple, easy-to-read, useful collection of data that should help you get what you need.

---

[189]www.businessweek.com/the_thread/blogspotting/archives/2008/03/yahoos_raghavan.html

From a content producer's perspective, this requires you to make a lot of changes to your perception of what matters, especially if you believe the value of your content is the site that houses it.

ADVERTISING ON THE PAGE PALES

If someone is seeking how-to videos on playing the cello, and you have a cello podcast (e.g., www.cellojourney.com) relying on a wraparound of Google AdSense for bandwidth and beer money, your video might now have legs to land on a search results page *sans advertising*. In cases where you've built ads and affiliate programs all over your site, a search like the one Yahoo's Prabhakar Raghavan is envisioning might leave your ads in the dust.

GOOD CONTENT WILL BE FOUND

On the other hand, if it benefits you or your organization to get your content out to more places, then, as Powered's Aaron Strout[190] pointed out to me, this is a case where excellent content will suddenly have *more* visibility, and you'll be heard by more folks. If you look at it another way, asking users/searchers to jump through hoops to connect with what they're searching for doesn't sound all that appealing, does it? You can watch a video pretty much anywhere. You can read anywhere. Content

---

[190]http://tinyurl.com/273ujz

was built to be let loose, even if this means changing the business model a bit.

Producing great content and this new way of searching go hand in hand, but it also means that you have to consider tweaking your content for this new world. Include ways for people to get back to your main site, including links, directly *in* the content you're creating. For text, consider adding links back to your main site in each post. For audio, make sure to read out your URL at the end (maybe near the beginning, too) of every post. Ditto with video.

GET A JUMP ON THE COMPETITION

If you look at this as an opportunity, you can see all kinds of ways that having quality microcontent and using appropriate microformats would be a great way to deliver portable value that might catapult you ahead of other search efforts.

For the average user, it's worth considering how you might interact in this new space; think ahead about how you present *your* brand in a world where semantic data might change the search game in a big way.

So, what do you think? Is your data ready? Are you?

50

Social Media—Talk Is Cheap for Businesses

There's lots of talk about social media. Tons. The echo is nearly deafening at this point. Freedom. Openness. We have powerful tools to communicate. We are the media. It's all about the conversation. We talk about this all the time. At the same time, more people are just starting to get into this, so it's all new and exciting and fresh again. Businesses are starting to ask, "Hey, is there something here, or is this just another billable item, like when we used to pay for someone to build brochureware for us?" Businesses are asking how this stuff all threads into their world, their terms. They're asking how we're going to change their bottom line, deliver something to their top line, make this all worth it.

Do you have an answer for them? Here are some thoughts that lead down the path of helping businesses understand the value proposition.

Collaboration Tools—Internal

Things like blogs, podcasting, Utterli, Twitter, wikis, and more unified tools such as JiveSoftware and BaseCamp[191] are useful

---

[191]www.camphq.com

for internal processes and collaboration. I believe they are better than the tools most enterprises uses to communicate about a project. I believe the implementation of such tools is simple, requires little or no infrastructure (depending on security requirements), and most often can be cloud-operated, depending on comfort levels. These can be used in a number of ways:

- Status messaging
- Informational training
- Project management
- Knowledge management

SOCIAL NETWORKING TOOLS—WHITE LABEL

For organizations that have a large customer base, a large partner base, or any circumstance where the audience is already fairly well defined (more often in B2C spaces), building a social network around your community such that you manage and maintain all aspects of the experience is simple. Tools like Ning and Awareness Networks[192] and several others[193] exist, can be implemented inexpensively, and deliver some potential value to a mixture of uses:

- Lead generation
- Customer service

---

[192] www.AwarenessNetworks.com
[193] www.web-strategist.com/blog/2007/02/12/list-of-white-label-social-networking-platforms/

- Community development
- Product development (Lego Mindstorm, Dell IdeaStorm, My Starbucks Idea)
- Data collection (profiles and usage might drive more marketing insight)
- Recruiting

SOCIAL NETWORKING TOOLS— COMMERCIAL AND CONSUMER

MySpace, Facebook, LinkedIn, Bebo,[194] Orkut,[195] and others are all places where people gather. As such, one might use these areas as a place to market, a place to recruit, a place to understand the marketplace, a place to build relationships without strings (I know that's crazy talk, but hey). Have they proven fertile ground for advertising? Not for B2B. How about for B2C? The results are mixed. Ad spending is shifting online. GM announced recently that it's moving toward spending one-third of its ad budget online in the next little while. How much of that will show up in MySpace? Not clear.

BLOGGING, PODCASTING, VIDEO, GETTING THE WORD OUT

Blogging, I believe, is one of the best-use (maybe easiest) cases to support. There's the customer service angle (e.g., how Lionel

---

[194]www.Bebo.com
[195]www.Orkut.com

Menchaca really shifted public opinion of Dell with the Direct2-Dell blog). Bill Marriott (of the hotel world) keeps a decent blog.[196] There's a value to convincing companies to blog if they are willing to listen to a few suggestions:

- Write genuine, conversational content that is not just "me, me, me."
- Put the passionate person in charge of writing, not just the boss.
- Enable comments and be willing to engage in uncomfortable discussions (with a reasonable comments policy in place).
- Respond and comment on other people's blogs often.

Podcasting has some great applications, both in audio and video. The infrastructure and the production effort for both are inexpensive compared to traditional audio and video means. People are expecting more of a YouTube experience than a movie theater experience, and the more personal and direct the material, the better people relate. Businesses are learning how video can sweeten the experience. Take a look at Standout Jobs,[197] a company working heavily with video to create quality job recruiting and placement services.

Traditional media has flooded its way into podcasting. Check out the Apple iTunes store and you'll see it. Count in any section how many mainstream or mainstream-derivative products

---

[196]www.blogs.marriott.com/

[197]http://StandoutJobs.com

there are in the featured area compared to independents and you'll get an easy snapshot. Yet, for businesses, there's still a value there to pursue due to cheap production and cheap distribution opportunities.

THE STAFFING ISSUES

Where does one put a corporate blogger? Marketing? IT? Customer service? Product development? It depends, yet that's a question when it comes down to figuring out payroll, HR, reporting structure, and what comes next. How does one *measure* the effectiveness of this? Oh, go ahead. Tell me you know. There are *some* numbers. Lionel Menchaca from Dell talked about the negative perception rating as a key metric tracked by Dell during his blogging efforts (which Lionel helped reduce some 30 percent or more).

Oh, and good luck asking for a resume that will include the appropriate background for this. Where do bloggers or community managers or podcasters show their experience? They can *demonstrate* their capabilities, but they can't exactly point to a past role (well, most can't) and say, "Here's where I shot video for Rocketboom."[198] Does this make it harder to recruit? And are there really HR teams out there looking for social media types, or is this coming straight from the product management skunkworks fund?

Here's a square-peg, round-hole situation. If you're the community manager, you're in a position where it's part customer

---

[198]www.Rocketboom.com

service, part PR, part support, and part product development. You're at once the customer advocate and the rah-rah person for the company. And where do you get your training? To whom do you report? How does anyone give you a metric to cover what you do in a day.

If you're in the tech space, do you send your community manager to conferences? It's not business development. It's not lead generation (as such). Yet finance departments are receiving expense reports from people traveling to conferences just to do some brand exposure. How long will that last, if there's nothing to measure on the other end of it?

Starting to get the picture?

YOUR PART IN ALL THIS—IF YOU'RE THINKING BUSINESS

If you're looking at this from a "working with businesses" per-spective, I have a few things to say. You're going to have to address all that stuff up top and a bunch more. You're going to have to know how to convince corporate IT departments to crack open parts of the firewall. You're going to have to help write job descriptions that explain what these jobs do for these businesses. You're going to have to get a whole lot less vague on the value you're bringing to the table as a thought leader and strategist in this space. You're not going to have an easy walk in the door of a not-so-Silicon-Valley place as a blogger or podcaster, so start upping your ante on skills and perspective.

WHERE ARE THE PEACE AND LOVE AND KOOL-AID?

There are tons. *Tons*. Just decide to take that blue pill. If you do, that's cool. There's lots of fun to be had in making media, communicating, sharing your voice, reaching out, and establishing new relationships. People do it all the time, and it matters.

BACK TO THE RED PILL

If you're going to present yourself as a business professional showing the value of these tools to companies, step up your game. Do. Make. Learn. And build the appropriate human interface between what these businesses understand and what you're offering. It's there. You *can* do it. You have to be working at it from that perspective.

51

The Community Ecosystem

There really aren't many secrets about how things work in social media. There are skills to learn, and then there are human traits to relearn. Yet when people jump into this space and try to get results for their efforts, they're sometimes surprised and frustrated. Sometimes, when we're rushed, we forget the "nice" parts of things, yet in a community ecosystem, that's what will drive your results. Here are some thoughts.

CONTRIBUTE WHERE YOU CAN

Brian Solis[199] is an upstanding member of this new world. He's been in it for more than 10 years with his forward-thinking new PR company, FutureWorks. When Brian comes to a gathering, he brings his monster camera and a great eye, and he snaps *tons* of photos. But it's what comes next that proves my point. Brian shares his photos on Flickr, and he shares them with Creative Commons permissions so that you can pretty much use his photos for anything, provided you give him credit.

You can contribute *somewhere* in the community ecosystem. Maybe it's by sharing your photos. Maybe it's by offering small-business tips[200] for budding freelancers. Maybe it's by offering presentation advice.[201] Wherever you can, offer up (easily and for free) stuff that *you* can bring to the community.

COMMUNICATE WHEN YOU CAN

The Zulu greet each other by saying, "*Sawubona*," translated literally as, "I see you." It means, "I know that you're there

---

[199]http://briansolis.com/
[200]www.smallbizsurvival.com/2008/03/checklists-for-starting-your-first.html
[201]http://pistachioconsulting.com/

and I acknowledge you as another person." The response is, "*Ngikhona*," literally, "I am here."

Visiting people's web sites and/or just reading their RSS feeds isn't enough all the time. Make a point of commenting, of saying, "I see you." Sometimes (okay, often) I receive e-mail from people saying that they don't get any comments on their web sites, and they wonder why they should bother. *Many* people have the feeling they're out in the wild doing nothing important. You might be contributing to this feeling by not commenting, even occasionally, on some of the places you visit.

When you can, share a little "I see you" with the places where you interact. Because it will matter. It does come back to you. People do care.

CREATE WHAT YOU CAN

Participating, building, and creating are all possible with these tools and with this way that people are seeing the landscape of work. We have the potential to be more connected to each other than ever before. And from this, we now have the opportunity to lighten the burden of others by creating things that others can use.

Some ways to create are to build things for people who don't necessarily have the skills, but who have a need that you can fulfill. Another way is to add value by contributing to an existing project. Other times, it's as simple as organizing a gathering (either online or in the real world) of people with similar interests, such that you can help catalyze the conversations and the shared experience. Create. Make. Do. And share.

THE COMMUNITY ECOSYSTEM ISN'T FOREMOST ABOUT MONEY

It's not a question of freely sharing hippies versus moneymaking capitalists. These things I'm mentioning work both ways. You can do these things in the space where it's just "nice," and you can do these things in the space where the value comes back to the company in some other way. That's not the point, because the skills required to contribute to this ecosystem are necessary in both places. In fact, they're interchangeable.

How are *you* contributing? Where are you communicating? What are you creating? Come see us.

Social Media Starter Moves for Freelancers

Opportunities for entrepreneurial spirits, freelancers, and consultants are on the rise. A weak economy (such as we're experiencing in the United States right now) is one reason, but another is the flexibility such employees offer companies who might not have the resources (or want the overhead) related to taking on full-time staff for certain roles. And yet, with so much competition for attention, how can you rise above the fray to be not only seen but selected for the opportunities you seek? Here are some thoughts on the matter.

FIRST: PROFESSIONALISM, OR NOT

Before you even start in on this whole thing, determine whether you're a fun-loving soul looking to make a few extra bucks on the side or someone seeking to build a sustainable stream of revenue to support yourself and possibly a family. If the former, skip pretty much everything I'm about to tell you. If the latter, read on.

YOUR BLOG, YOUR STOREFRONT

If you're in the business of delivering a service (coding skills, design, marketing expertise, sales, etc.), there's a whole lot of factory work that you do that's not easily displayed. Yet you need a storefront to "productize" what you do (tip of the hat to my friend, Liz Strauss,[202] for talking with me about her passion for turning what someone does into a product).

ADS, SIDEBARS, AND WIDGETS

Before we get down to brass tacks, let's do some cleanup work:

- Kill random ads. If you're a successful freelancer, why are you trying to make beer money with your site?

---

[202]www.successful-blog.com/1/get-unambiguous-and-get-more-customers/

- Kill random widgets. To simplify, tidy your blog so that it looks clean and professional (you can have fun and be engaging, but consider your buying audience).
- Kill the calendar thingy. *No one* navigates by it.
- Look for useless widgets. Your "phases of the moon" graphic slows down your blog and diffuses your intent.
- Enable comments, and make it as easy as possible.

POSTING IDEAS

Now, let's talk about your blog as your business engine:

- Start writing posts that cover your space and establish you as the thought leader, only humble. Be the "thought learner."
- *Stop* writing posts that are horribly off-topic, or at least keep it down to a 10-to-1 ratio of on- versus off-topic.
- Link to other blogs that cover your space as well, and say complimentary things when you can. This is an "abundance mentality" space. Sure, there are plenty of folks who aren't "the best," like you, but when you say it, it makes you sound cheap.
- Make sure your passion shows through. That's what people buy.
- The more you explore *new* ideas in your space and, furthermore, explain right out in the open how people can make money, reduce costs, whatever, the more business you'll bring in.

ABOUT AND CONTACT

Make your "About" page read like a great (somewhat brief) testimonial. People want to know first and foremost what you can do for them. Write it as if the person reading it is asking, "I like Sonia. How do I work with her?"

If you can, include a recent headshot. If you don't have a great one, buy a throwaway digital camera for $20 and shoot shots of your head until you get a good one. It's not *that* hard. Don't do one of those scary Glamour Shots (no offense to the organization) or those grownup versions of school photos with the weird cloud background. Here's one spot where you can be somewhat creative in what you put up there. Make it somehow reflect what you're hoping to portray.

Put your *contact* information everywhere. On the main page. On the About page. On the contact page. Make it really easy for people to reach you and do business with you.

PROMOTING YOUR BLOG

Here's a quick list of ways to get a little more love and attention for your blog:

- Add your blog URL to your signature file for your e-mail.
- Add your blog URL to your LinkedIn profile, your Twitter account, your Facebook profile.
- Use Facebook tools like Flog Blog, Blog Friends, and Feedheads. They all expand your reach.
- Get a Flickr account.

- Join a few blog directories (Google for these).
- Share links via e-mail with folks.
- Use FeedBurner and put a "subscribe by e-mail" option on your blog.

COMMUNITY BUILDING: BEYOND YOUR BLOG

Become active on other people's blogs. Build relationships with other people in your space. If you're a freelance musician, get really active on people's MySpace pages, their blogs, their fan forums. Be where the people you need to reach are, and then be part of that scene. Some suggestions:

- Twitter. Say what you will, but Twitter is a way to get to know other people, mostly in the tech scene, but you'd be surprised (e.g., *tons* of knitters on Twitter).
- Ning. There are plenty of groups and shared interests in this white-label social network platform, and more and more people are using it.
- Facebook. Groups there can be active and/or can go quiet fairly quickly (my experience, overall).
- Yahoo! Groups. Don't forget this very simple method of reaching active communities of people.
- Update. Laura[203] and Jeremy[204] said lots of people enjoy great community (and business!) from LinkedIn.

---

[203]http://notanemployee.com/
[204]http://jeremyvaught.com/

REAL-TIME SOCIAL GATHERINGS

Now more than ever, opportunities to meet and connect with people in the real world are important and valuable for your ability to meet and do business with others. You don't have to go in like old-school networkers, eager to suck in as many handshakes and business cards as humanly possible in the shortest amount of time, but you *should* consider how this will relate to your strategy of building business relationships that might result in appropriate work opportunities for you. To that end, some thoughts.

- Conferences are great (I produce them for a living, so of course I'll say that). You get to know lots of people in a short amount of time while, hopefully, being educated on topics that matter to you. Check Upcoming.org and Eventful.com for lists of conferences that relate to your space.

- Make decent-looking business cards. Your hack-job Staples photocopy cards are quaint, but they immediately tell me that you are unprepared. (I've been this guy twice over the past two years.) And, by *decent-looking,* I mean that "clever" only seems interesting while I'm shaking your hand. Cards that tell me how to reach you and how you and I might do business are awesome. Provide your cell number, no matter what.

- Write some great blog content in the days leading up to an event, so that when people read your business card and see your blog prominently displayed there (you knew that, right?), they'll check you out and realize you're the right person to hire for that blog redesign project.

- Go to more than just conferences. Attend social media gatherings, local events, meetups. Don't be afraid. *Lots* of new folks show up. If you can, find a Twitter user or a blogger or someone you can learn about ahead of time. Build the relationship *before* you go, and that will help with some of the anxiety.

RICH MEDIA—VIDEO AND AUDIO

If you have the time and inclination, make a podcast or video blog about the space you're passionate about. Want to hear a great marketing podcast? Check out Marketing Over Coffee.[205] I'd hire those two guys in a heartbeat to train a traditional team to do new stuff. Want to know about a great personal development trainer? Check out The Bigg Success Show.[206]

Video? Gary Vaynerchuk[207] is the poster child for demonstrating authenticity while building trust in his personal and business brand. For another great example, check out what Ben Yoskowitz is doing at Standout Jobs. Learn from that.

Video and audio are great tools to build up an experience with your potential audience. It gives people a sense of how you might be in person. Even though you *could* edit the life out of your media so that you'd show up as polished and professional, it's one more wall coming down between a no and a yes.

---

[205]www.marketingovercoffee.com

[206]www.biggsuccess.com

[207]www.garyvaynerchuk.com

Some might ask whether this opens people up for potential discrimination. Absolutely. I have no doubt. That was what kept LinkedIn from putting up optional profile pictures for a long time, too, but after a while, it's a question of whether or not you just want to put yourself out there and call it good. That's your call. My take? They're going to meet you at some point, right?

STRATEGY POINT: GIVE TO GET

In the world of freelancing, my take is that the best way to build relationships and get more business is to help other people get business. This has nothing to do with social media. It has everything to do with humans. If you're helpful, and if you're out there giving people ideas, tools, insights, and passing on connections where you think they'll do the most good, you'll likely be in *someone's* mind when something good comes along.

Part of this goes into the space of thinking about "free." Don't be so eager to get paid for every little thing you do. (Disclaimer: I'm teetering on dirt broke most of the time, so maybe this isn't sound *financial* advice.) I believe that there are lots of "long tail" opportunities out there. It just becomes your duty to decide which ones are eventually going to pay off and which ones you should stop doing.

That's my sermon on "free."

LAST, ASK FOR THE SALE

If you're not out there *looking* for customers, don't moan that you don't have many. Don't be overly aggressive and barracuda-like, but by all means, if someone's courting you a little in the comments section or the e-mail section, ask if there's something you can help that person work on. It's not rude. It's not overly aggressive (okay, maybe on first contact, but if you've been playing e-mail footsie, then go for it).

If you're saying you want to use your blog and social media tools to get business, ask for business. I promise, the results will improve on that front the moment you get over that glitch.

SUMMARY

If you're a freelancer hoping to use social media to get work, here's a quick summary:

- Make your blog your storefront.
- Kill all the extraneous stuff from it.
- Write posts that establish your experience and abilities in the industry.
- Write other posts that promote other people, too.
- Contribute beyond the walls of your blog.
- Attend real-time events, too.
- Consider whether you want to add audio and video.
- Give to get.
- Ask for the sale.

This was how I built New Marketing Labs. With the help of my business partners, Stephen and Nick Saber, and with my starting team, Justin Levy and Colin Browning, we launched our site by following a lot of these moves. I still do the same things for my personal business, www.chrisbrogan.com, and my new company, Human Business Works.

Making a Business from Social Media

Who's making a business from social media? Audio and video producers are, for the most part, scraping by, give or take a few notables (several of whom are being paid from venture capital money). Bloggers are making money in varying degrees, depending on their advertising and/or consulting opportunities. I'm going to leave the entertainment category out of this discussion for that reason (though you're welcome to argue it back in). So, who's really making a business from social media?

EARLY ADOPTERS: ADVERTISING, PR, AND MARKETING

First to market with actual paying jobs in social media are public relations and marketing firms. Why? Because if you squint your eyes, the tools are the same thing: a means for communicating professionally. Is that wrong? I don't think so, provided we don't lose ground with regard to how these new tools rehumanize technology-assisted communication.

Using social media for viral advertising is popular, but mostly because it's low-cost, low-barrier technology that permits folks to get a message across through different channels. Will that last? I can't see why we'd go back to $100,000 spots when we can create the media and distribute it for free, especially where the world is shifting to those free methods, too.

BUSINESS USERS

I'm not sure what department an *internal* corporate social media practitioner would fall into. Project management makes sense, because inside the firewall, these tools facilitate collaboration, status messages, data sharing, and other uses that would work well for facilitating projects. Product management and R&D might adopt the tools as well, but there probably wouldn't be a predefined role for someone who simply knows how to use the tools.

COMPARING THE TWO MOST LIKELY BUSINESSES

On one side we have obvious jobs: PR, marketing, and advertising. On the other hand, we have a potential role for someone inside daring companies who seek to use the tools internally, OR, more likely, the tools we're talking about will become commonplace and distributed to all the employees.

Which makes more sense? On one side, you have a mountain of communications companies hoping to adapt quickly.

On the other side, you have businesses that aren't as motivated to change their internal processes. Will there be a point where businesses take back their external arms for outreach to their customers? In a world where companies talk directly to their customers, the media, and prospects, will the business of communications go in-house?

NOT NECESSARILY A PRIMARY BUSINESS

We're all jumping up and down and excited about social media and what these tools can do for us. *What*, exactly, do these tools do for us that translates directly into a business? My answer: For lots of people, they don't.

Looking for a career in social media is like seeking a career in e-mail. Instead, use these skills to cultivate another ability of yours. If you're a salesperson, use social media tools to build leads, understand needs, spread the word about your products. If you're a nonprofit professional, you've already figured this out and no doubt use these tools to aid in awareness, fund-raising, communication, and more.

Instead of focusing on how these tools will become a career, focus on how you can equip others with these tools. *That*, I believe, is the business in the short term. But keep in mind that it *will* be the short term.

54

Make Your Blog Design Work for You

Everything I've done with my blog design is intentional. I'm not saying that my blog design is perfect, and I certainly have other things I'd like to do with it in the future, but I want to share with you some thoughts about blog design, starting with my blog, then showing some design ideas from other sites as well. Why should blog design matter? Because you want your blog to serve the purpose you've built it to serve.

FIRST, KNOW THE GOAL

The goal of my blog is to provide you with a body of work on social software and the strategies surrounding it. One part of that goal is the hope that my work gives you starting points to launch out and do this on your own. The other part of the goal is to inform people, who need more than I've posted, that I'm available to help them with their specific needs. What do you think? Does my site match my goal?

What's the goal of your blog?

CONSIDER A THIN HEADER

When building the redesign of www.chrisbrogan.com, I wanted the header at the top to be very thin. I wanted you to be able to see as much of my page layout as possible instead of a huge static graphical banner at the top.

Check out Copyblogger and ProBlogger. Brian Clark and Darren Rowse have me beat on thin headers. They even have functionality alongside their names in the headers. Commercial concerns like TechCrunch and GigaOM[208] have ads at the top, but note how GigaOM handles ads. He's got it wrapped into the header, saving space. For whatever reason, that design makes the ad seem less blatant to me. You?

YOUR "ABOUT" PAGE MATTERS

My About[209] page starts with a picture of me. (I want a very current pic all the time, because it helps you find me at conferences.) The page also gives you a bio that tells you what I'm passionate about. If you look further at it, my About page is also serving suggestions regarding how you can work with me. I want you thinking the whole time you're reading it, "Oh, look! I'm in the market for someone to help my company figure out our social media strategy, and Chris does that!" That's not by accident.

Valeria Maltoni's About page[210] has an even more professional feel to it. (I'm taking notes now.) And she uses a picture to make sure we know who she is.

---

[208]http://GigaOM.com

[209]http://chrisbrogan.com/about

[210]http://conversationagent.typepad.com/about.html

Brian Clark's About page[211] for Copyblogger starts with the essence of the blog, then talks about him, and the message there reinforces that his blog is about the work, not about him.

What does your About page look like? What more will I learn about you and about your goals with your blog?

YOUR SIDEBAR(S)

Sidebars are my personal pet peeve. I want the things in them to be relevant to the experience, useful to the user, and pertinent to the information at hand. To that end, the first three things on my sidebar are the RSS subscription link, my newsletter[212] subscription link (which is different content than my blog), and a "get this blog by e-mail" box. Why? Because my number one goal is to have you connected to this experience on a continual basis.

Most sidebars start with the subscription opportunities. I noted that Copyblogger, ProBlogger, and Conversation Agent all display their RSS subscriber count. I didn't have this on my site for a while, but then realized there's one piece of value in it: It shows that more than a few people consider your site useful for information. Don't feel like you have to wait until you have 10,000 subscribers to put up that button, and don't feel weird if you have only 100. More than two is probably good. (Note: It took me eight years to get my first 100 subscribers).

---

[211]www.copyblogger.com/copywriting/
[212]http://chrisbrogan.com/newsletters

ADS, OR NO ADS?

You can certainly use ads on your site. Some folks do it very tastefully. Where it becomes a problem to me is when you've laden your page with so many ads that I can no longer read the content easily, and heaven forbid that you have me clicking on something that I don't know is an ad. Spamming your audience is unpleasant.

Should sites have ads? Sure. Why not? But be clear about what your intentions are, and try your hardest to make the ads pertinent to your audience.

What's your take on this one?

BLOGROLLS, OR NO?

Some sites have a blogroll (where folks can see all the other blogs you endorse or don't endorse). It's a personal preference.

Do you use one? Have people commented positively or negatively about it?

FONTS AND TEXT COLORS

I like readable blogs. I like artsy design, but I also want people to be able to read it. When I looked around, there was a real mix to what people used on their sites for font and colors. I prefer a serif font (text that has curvy parts), whereas others may prefer sans serif (more modern-looking).

PICTURES AND VIDEO AND RICH MEDIA

I love video blogs. I love photo blogs. In my case, I use my blog in multiple ways, so I consider it a text blog with pictures, or a text blog with video. If yours is specific to one of these other purposes, you might consider designs that further highlight your main purpose.

If you're blogging in text, consider using photos and video. They add something to a reader's experience. You'll note that I often put up a photo alongside my posts. I use Flickr's vast assortment of Creative Commons–licensed photos, created by the world to be used with proper attribution. (Learn more about that on Flickr's Creative Commons site.[213])

SUMMARY

To sum up what I want you to consider when thinking about your blog design:

- What's the goal of your blog? Does your design serve that goal?
- Consider a thin header.
- Make your About page useful.
- Keep your sidebar functional.
- If you have ads, keep them tasteful and unobtrusive.
- Consider how blogrolls affect your design.
- Do your fonts and their color help your readers?
- Should you add rich media, such as photos and video, to your blog?

---

[213]http://flickr.com/creativecommons

Feel free to share designs you think work well in the comments section of my blog at http://chrisbrogan.com/comments-from-101, and we can talk about *your* blog, too, if people feel like sharing.

Social Media Starter Moves for Real Estate

Disclaimer right up front: I'm not in the real estate biz, so I'll write this from the perspective of what I've observed and what might be useful. Some real *real estate pro can come and fix this on his or her own blog, and it'll likely be better. Why would I ever let a simple thing like inexperience get in the way of sharing my opinion?*

SHOW ME THE HOUSE

The first and most obvious thing I think the real estate world can (and should) be doing is buying video cameras and shooting their own walk-throughs. You don't have to be a pro. You *do* have to know how not to make something look horrible, but that comes with trial and error.

PICK UP A VIDEO CAMERA

If you don't yet own a video camera, here are a few thoughts:

- Most still cameras have a video feature, and that's nearly good enough.
- The Flip camera is the *easiest* and often the least expensive video camera to use.
- Kodak's new Zi8 (and related) models have more flexibility than the Flip, but are a bit more complicated as a trade-off.

EDITING

Now, to actually *do* it, you have two options: Learn how to edit things easily in iMovie (Mac) or Windows Media Maker (PC), or pay someone to edit what you shoot. Benefits of the former are that you can edit when you need it and your time is all you pay. Benefits of the latter are that the editing pros are good at what they do, will save you time, and will know what to do next. The drawback of hiring someone is that it costs money and you have no control over when your files are returned, depending on how professional your person is.

POSTING THE VIDEO

The last step to putting up a video is to find hosting for the video so that you can then embed it on your blog. YouTube makes sense for two reasons. One, it's easy, and most people can navigate it. Two, it becomes a second market for your homes if you've added captions that show how to contact you.

If you want a different look and feel from YouTube, you can try Blip.tv, Brightcove, Vimeo, Viddler, and a gazillion other companies who host video and have a nifty player.

WAYS YOUR BLOG WILL HELP

First, blogging about certain properties you're hoping to move will give you an obvious potential return, but that might be limited. Instead, think of what buyers and sellers might need to know, and what they might need to know about you. You're likely going to weigh this information heavily on the sell side, and that's okay, so make your web site a great place to learn about things like curb appeal and how to declutter a home for better showability. Give people ideas that have added thousands to the sale price of your clients' homes.

TESTIMONIALS

People are so itchy about asking for testimonials. Don't be. Ask. Ask your clients with whom you've had a great business experience to comment. Want to get really edgy? Be willing to post someone's negative comments about your business with them, and don't be defensive. Instead, just thank them.

THE SECRET SAUCE

As a media maker, you can do things that will add to one's impressions of a potential new home. You can shoot video of the general neighborhood, add Flickr photos of some selling points of the town, record audio reports of people's general feelings about the town. Can you imagine the impact that might make? You could potentially take a normal-looking house and demonstrate the value of the home's setting through media.

Will everyone care? No. Will you have a chance to reach more folks? I'm betting yes.

56

How Do Realtors Demonstrate Community?

Through a conversation in Twitter, I happened across Life in Bonita Springs, a blog by Chris Griffith (aka @Twitterzilla). The first post that caught my eye was a beautiful shot of a public area[214] called Coconut Point, with a really small dog in the foreground. The blog post was about a "small-dogs-only social." Wow, I thought. Now that's something you don't see every day. It got me thinking.

---

[214]http://lifeinbonitasprings.com/a-little-something-at-coconut-point-today/

REALTY CAN BENEFIT A *LOT* WITH THESE TOOLS

There are lots of ways social media can be applied, but look at real estate. If your job is to sell community, you can do lots of things. Create a video blog of interviews of people in the community you're trying to sell into. Build an events page or a community site where people can gather, share their stories, post events, and express themselves. Take mountains of photos on Flickr, showing off the best in community art, as well as some of the finer homes.

HOW DOES IT ALL TIE TOGETHER?

If I'm reading a community or realty blog, how will you convert me from a blog reader into a home buyer? What are the right ways to convert me gently? For example, on Chris Griffith's blog, I see the sidebar has ways to connect me to her. If I'm an RSS subscriber, I won't ever see that, and there's nothing in the post to connect me to business.

This is great if the only goal is to keep people in the community aware of what's going on in the community, but if another goal of the blog is to sell homes, is there a way you could gently convert me?

Or should you?

57

Social Media Starter Moves for Entertainers

Twitter brought me a really special gift a month or two back in the shape of Grace Nikae.[215] She's a concert pianist who is exploring the use of social media to build relationships with her audience and fans of music. In imagining how I'd advise a professional entertainer to use social media, I doubt that I could find someone more accomplished at reaching into social media than Grace. Let's explore a bit.

BLOG BEHIND THE SCENES

Grace has a great blog called Stretching Intervals,[216] which is a perfect mix of what goes on behind the scenes and information about what it's like to be a pianist. She writes posts that are worthy of being full-fledged journal articles, yet they're very approachable and readable.

By blogging what's on her mind, Grace gives a glimpse of what it's like to be a busy creative and professional to her fans,

---

[215]http://gracenikae.com/

[216]http://StretchingIntervals.gracenikae.com

aspiring pianists, professional women, and anyone else who wants to know.

SHARE A LITTLE

Grace provides links to her YouTube videos, to photos on Flickr, and to other little tidbits all through her web site. It gives you a sense of what she's about, her style, and a peek at what you're missing if you don't go to her concerts. Sure, there's a store and other things you'd expect from a professional musician, but if you fault her for that, you're crazy. After watching and listening to her YouTube videos, I plan on picking up her debut solo album, *Fantasies*.

STRETCH OUT

Grace also maintains a presence on Facebook, MySpace, Twitter, and a few other social sites, and though it's a bit challenging to maintain it all, I've seen her have conversations on Twitter, and I've been privy to several thoughtful comments on my blog. She's managing to find a little time to cover some thoughts and have conversations with people well outside her world as a pianist.

Will it be fruitful? I guess Grace will have to tell us in several months whether all this social media brought her a different experience than before she started using it.

FOR ENTERTAINERS

Musicians and comics know that MySpace is a viable place to meet new audiences, build community, and promote your performances. Dane Cook made a good chunk of his career's launch off MySpace's mechanisms. Facebook isn't as effective for performers, but I know that more folks are coming over to try it out. Twitter? It's not exactly teeming with celebrities, but savvy folks like Grace Nikae are trying it out, so we'll see how that turns out. My advice?

- Do this social media yourself. Don't use an assistant.
- Communication is a two-way street. Just blurting out your calendar isn't going to win you friends.
- Be just as much about other people as you are about yourself.
- Give us peeks behind the scenes.
- Share a little something.
- Don't get lost in all this stuff, as your real product is your performances.

We have lots of talented and upcoming performers and entertainers in our midst, several of whom already use these tools to great effect. Is it having an impact on their careers? Will these tools benefit the mainstream stars as much as they do those who have a built-in appeal to the social media set? Time will tell.

Social Media Starter Moves for Entrepreneurs

I tend to talk from the perspective of a user of technology, but I am writing this one for people who might be seeking to build new tools, to join the social software scene. I love entrepreneurs, and I enjoy the notion of building new, amazing things. But I do want you to think about this space, too.

If you're *not* building a social network or platform, stick around. I want *you* to tell folks your thoughts, too.

THE PLATFORMS WE'RE USING

I'm definitely not going to list every social network and social media tool, but I do want you to understand a bit about *how* we're using these tools, so I'll mention a few.

- Facebook. Not just for kids anymore. The grown-ups I know use this service for roughly the same thing: connecting with people they already know and making some new connections.

- LinkedIn. Business social networking—the top of the heap. It's getting a *little* more interesting, because of its status stream and the redesign.
- Twitter. Not everyone's on there, but we're more on there than Pownce and Jaiku. Why? It's not because it's better. It's just because we're all still there, because it's simple, because it meets a lot of needs.
- Flickr. We're sharing photos on Flickr and SmugMug.
- YouTube. We're sharing video on YouTube and Blip.tv and a few dozen smaller places.
- Digg. We're getting news from Digg and Reddit and SlashDot, and there are lots of new upstarts for specific niches. We seem to like these sites because they let the crowd vote on what's newsworthy to the United States as a niche.

That's some of what we're interested in. You'll certainly want to add places and tools into the comments section of my blog at http://chrisbrogan.com/comments-from-101 so that we can bring those to attention, too.

THE MARKETPLACE OVERALL

I'd say the barrier to getting me to join a new social network is getting higher and higher. If you're doing a business network, I'm already using LinkedIn. If you're building a place for friends to connect, Facebook, in all its annoyance, still handles that satisfactorily, and Twitter handles it excellently.

What comes next for networks? Velvet rope. Lots of it. I think the next step (and this was once prophesied by Eric Rice[217] somewhere) is something closer to an antisocial network or, more accurately, a professional social network. Want to see a top-shelf example? Check out Sermo,[218] a social network for physicians. I met with Daniel Palestrant, the founder, recently, and he's a smart cookie. He's got a great product and he knows it.

What about tools?

SOCIAL MEDIA TOOLS

There are lots of overlap experiences going on at the moment. For instance, there's an entire social information aggregation space, showing all different spins. There's Lijit for search, FriendFeed for aggregation, and then maybe a dozen variations on the theme thereafter. Check out Louis Gray's site[219] for *tons* of these types of apps.

There's BlogTalkRadio and Utterli offering phone-to-podcast experiences with different twists. (I'm friendly with both companies, and they're both full of great people.)

In blogging software and content platforms, we have WordPress, Drupal, Tumblr, Blogger, Joomla,[220] TypePad, LiveJournal,[221] Posterous, and another million opportunities.

---

[217]http://ericrice.com/

[218]www.sermo.com

[219]www.louisgray.com

[220]www.Joomla.org

[221]www.LiveJournal.com

There are *many* tools. So then, what is the barrier to entry with either another tool or network?

High. Challenging. Difficult.

WHAT TO DO WITH IT ALL

Build your own dial tone. Use these tools to build up platforms of conversation and to talk with people about what matters to you. That's the real sauce. The tools are just what we need to move forward. It's what we do with it that counts.

Customer Service Needs New Channels . . . or Does It?

Michael Arrington opens this discussion[222] by sharing how Comcast responded faster to his complaints in Twitter than it

---

[222]www.techcrunch.com/2008/04/06/comcast-twitter-and-the-chicken-trust-me-i-have-a-point/

did to his customer service department phone calls. If I said nothing more and pushed "publish," a business owner should at least raise an eyebrow and ask, "Where are my customers? Do I have listening posts and responders there?"

Customer service exists on phones because the majority of people in most countries use and have access to a phone. But do *your* customers use phones as a primary source of contact? Do they use e-mail? Where are they? What are they using to communicate quickly?

In the 1990s, I worked in customer service, and eventually became manager of the local telephone company's 411 offices (which handle directory assistance calls). I have about six or seven years of frontline and management customer service experience, so I understand about handling times, about the cost balance, and so on.

But are there low-cost, flexible, measurable ways you could be improving your customer service channels by investigating and understanding where your customers are spending time and energy online? Absolutely.

For everyone? Definitely *not*. But I could probably name about 1,000 businesses who'd do better by having someone monitoring blogs, Twitter, and Facebook than they would by reducing handling time at a call center.

We wrote about this in more detail in *Trust Agents*. Frank Eliason, the guy who started Comcast Cares using Twitter, has sparked a revolution. The genie is out of the bottle. Customer service has moved into places like Twitter, and it will spread to many more platforms before it's finished. This will wreak havoc on your customer service metrics, on your call center management plans, and everything else. Yet it's the way things are being done.

What I Want a Social Media Expert to Know

Lots of people are throwing out the term *social media expert*. I had it as part of my About page on my blog, but now I've chosen to just say that I advise people. It's more accurate, because expertise is fairly fleeting out there right now. With that in mind, I've been thinking about things I want a so-called expert to know (and I want you to add to the following lists, or call me out if you disagree).

STRATEGIC
- Which department you think your role should fall into.
- How your role ties to marketing, PR, advertising, R&D, finance, HR, sales.
- What tasks you'd expect a community manager to perform, and how you would measure them.

- How you expect a company to engage in "the conversation," and what processes will go into place to make any of that matter.
- How to turn blog posts into business leads.
- How to listen and find where people are talking about you.
- Ways to report your weekly listening and community work to a very senior level person in a huge company that has about two minutes of time to hear your briefing.
- Know about 100 people in the space who are doing something. The more diverse the profession and location, the better.
- How to launch and operate a blogger outreach campaign.
- How to tie other media into social media as an integrated campaign.

TACTICAL

- How to install a blog (pick your software) on a hosted server.
- How to edit the sidebar to include a widget, an embed, or anything.
- How to create, edit, and post at least one other type of media besides text.
- At least five social network accounts active, including but not limited to LinkedIn, Yahoo! Groups, Facebook, Twitter, and YouTube.
- How to find and subscribe to a podcast *without* using iTunes.

- Five stats worth knowing for any blog or web site.
- How to structure a blog post so that humans *and* Google like it.

On Managing a Community

I wonder how most organizations are handling the role of community manager. I'm curious where a community manager reports. Marketing? HR? Customer service? I wonder how organizations are justifying the cost, and what they believe the role entails for level of effort. How are companies using the role in either direction?

Depending on the organization, I imagine the role of a community manager would be different, so I'm going to walk through what the role might entail for a media and events company (like mine[223]), and see what comes to mind. I could do the same for several other professions, but let's start here. Want to follow along? You can help me refine it in the comments section of my blog at http://chrisbrogan.com/comments-from-101.

---

[223]http://crosstechmedia.com/

STRATEGY

My strategy for a community manager would be to accomplish the following:

- Develop an awareness center for your industry (so you can listen and know what the community at large feels).
- Build a nonmarketing community outreach to deliver a voice for your organization to the industry.
- Engage the community you embrace, and facilitate learning and education from your organization's perspective and through relationships with other trusted organizations.

REPORTING STRUCTURE

My company is a fairly flat organizational structure. At my office, a community manager would report to me as the vice president of strategy and technology. Why? Because I'm charged with setting the tone and the look and feel of the content for all of our events. To me, the role at my organization would be to help me build on the customer experience.

DUTIES

My community manager (and here I'll use the feminine pronoun to save both of us the "he or she") would have accounts on the following platforms:

- LinkedIn
- Twitter

- Facebook
- Ning
- YouTube
- Google Reader

She would have responsibility to set up tracking and alerts for keywords specific to our industry, to subscribe to several industry blogs, podcasts, and video channels, and to subscribe to certain topic categories on YouTube.

She would comment on appropriate blogs. Not about our events, but about the topics at hand (the comments would have a URL back to her blog, for self-promotion on that front). Listening and commenting would be the bulk of her first three months' duties.

She would blog when she felt comfortable with the space.

If we decided to grow a Facebook or Ning community, she'd help facilitate good conversations there, too.

MEASUREMENTS

I'd measure my community manager on the following:

- Responsiveness to communications (blog comments, e-mails, Twitter messages, and forum threads) less than 24 hours, max.
- Number of *quality* blog posts read and shared via Google Reader.
- Number of meaningful comments (more than a few words, on topic, pertinent to the space) on appropriate blogs, videos, and other media per month.

- Overall quality of her Twitter stream (maybe a 60/30/10 mix of industry-related, personal @ comments, and off-topic).
- Engagement on our blog/community/network (number of subscribers, number of comments, number of links to other blogs from our community site).
- Number of quality blog posts and linking posts (probably a 40/60 split between original and linked, though some would argue for 30/70).
- Eventually, number of links from other sites to our blogs and media.

SUCCESS OF THE PROJECT

I'd think our community manager was a success if she accomplished the following through her efforts:

- Empower the listening ability of our organization to our community's needs and desires.
- Build an awareness of our organization through nonmarketing efforts, measured by favorable or at least nonnegative mentions on other blogs, forums, and in Twitter.
- Deliver a blog and/or media platform that's useful to the community at large and that grows in number of subscribers as well as engaged commenters.

Overall, I believe these efforts would be measured by an increase in attendance at our face-to-face and virtual events, an increase in subscriptions to our newsletter, and a larger blog commenting community. This would be a win to our organization, and would thus be worth the expense of another salaried employee.

62

Make Your LinkedIn Profile Work for You

LinkedIn is a professional network built around one's employment capabilities. It is often referred to (I believe somewhat incorrectly) as an online version of your CV or resume. People (e.g., Christopher S. Penn) who use LinkedIn expertly will be the first to say that this service is sorely underrated as a place to develop business, grow your capabilities, and promote your projects and opportunities. Here are some thoughts on amping up your LinkedIn presence.

WRITE TO BE READ

The first horror show I see when reading other people's LinkedIn profiles is that the writing is completely dry, as if robots are the only ones who will read them. Though you should write with robots in mind, this is still a human network, so write as if you want someone to actually read your profile. Here's the first paragraph of my summary:

> I show businesses how to use social media technologies for external community building and outreach, and for internal collaboration. I have over 10 years experience with social media and 16 years

experience in enterprise computing environments. I blend emerging tech knowledge with enterprise culture understanding.

You can tell what I do; you have a sense of what I'm hoping you want from me; you get a hint at my unique value proposition to businesses on this regard. It's not the best paragraph ever written, but it's definitely clear in explaining my core interests.

Make your summary explain, succinctly, why someone would want to tap your shoulder for business. If you're not sure why, that's another matter altogether. Read it aloud a few times to see how it sounds.

MAKE YOUR JOB DESCRIPTIONS WORK IN TWO WAYS

I want people who read my profile to see that I'm happily employed, that I work for a real company, and that my company has capabilities in certain areas. If you work for yourself, be clear about that, too. There's no shame in being a solo operator. Just be clear that you've chosen to build a profile to signal your professional capabilities, and write it in such a way that people understand where you sit.

Further, make sure that when people read your job description, they are thinking about how to put you to work on their issues. I state my company's primary functions in the first sentence of my current role, so that people can see what I'm bringing to the table alongside my own personal skills. Thus, my job description states what I'm doing, but also what I *can* do.

RECOMMENDATIONS ARE YOUR FRIENDS

I ask for recommendations all the time. I'm not shy about it. Why? Because I want other people's words to guide you to choosing me for your business needs. I want you not to have to take *my* word for it, but instead, to know what others have to say. Don't be shy about this, but also be very realistic about asking for recommendations.

I will not recommend people whose professional work I'm not familiar with enough to suggest to a close, personal friend. I'm willing to "friend" anyone, but I only recommend people I can vouch for professionally.

CONNECTION STRATEGIES

LinkedIn has an official opinion on connecting up with others. It recommends that you only connect with people you know well personally. You're welcome to take LinkedIn's opinion on that.

I've chosen to accept anyone who connects with me, and I've had to drop only one person, ever, for abusing that connection. Why? Because in my view, expanding my network means that *you* will find the person you need by searching through my network, and that I, at least in theory, can help you get to the person you need for your business efforts.

Your mileage may vary. I will do it my way, as most folks who connect with me eventually come calling to reach someone else that I've added, and I feel good every time I can be helpful.

SOME LAST THOUGHTS

- Check your contact settings. Be explicit about who you want connecting with you.
- Consider putting up a photo.
- Use the groups features, and find groups where you might want to contribute.
- Participate in the Q&A function to share your expertise (it's like free advertising, when done tastefully).
- Update at least every three months. Your role has changed. Make sure your profile reflects that.

63

Develop a Strong Personal Brand Online: Part 1

Gary Vaynerchuk could tell you that his personal brand is worth millions, but he's modest. My friend and PodCamp cofounder, Christopher S. Penn, often refers to branding by ZeFrank's definition: "an emotional aftertaste" (see the The Show with ZeFrank[224] episode). I have some thoughts on how you might

---

[224]www.zefrank.com/theshow/archives/2006/08/082906.html

develop a strong personal brand online, and what you might do with one after you build it.

WHY BUILD A PERSONAL BRAND?

You might already know the answer to this question. There are lots of answers, actually, depending on you, your needs, the way the world has shaped you. Let's look at just one answer.

The easiest answer is that you might want to be memorable, and you might want to transfer your real-world reputation to the online world. A strong personal brand is a mix of reputation, trust, attention, and execution. You might want to build a brand around being helpful (what I hope my brand means to you), or being a creative thinker (e.g., Hugh Macleod) or being a deal maker (Donald Trump), or being a showman (David Lee Roth), or whatever matters most to you—and what you are capable of sustaining.

A personal brand gives you the ability to stand out in a sea of similar products. In essence, you're marketing yourself as something different than the rest of the pack. Do you need this? I don't know. Do you like to be mixed in with the pack?

HINTS ABOUT BRAND IN GENERAL

What's the difference between Coke and Pepsi? There's a taste difference, for sure, but what does the brand signify? Tricky, eh? Both of those brands have spent billions so far telling us why they're different.

In some ways, the differentiator on brands is in what you deliver. What differentiates me from others might be the volume of useful content I deliver. I'm not sure. You tell me what makes me different. My answer would definitely vary from yours.

THE HUMAN SIDE OF BRAND

First of all, remember that branding isn't playing a role. Be yourself. It will become apparent rather quickly if you're being someone that you're not. Gary Vaynerchuk is the same guy, camera on or off. He may or may not tone himself down a bit when meeting new business partners, but I promise you that he reverts to being himself the moment someone's come to know what he's about.

Second, you may choose to use some kind of alias because you're afraid of the Internet and stalkers. That's great, except that your brand equity doesn't stretch to potential jobs, unless you go around explaining that you have a secret identity. As a guy who grew up reading comics, I'm okay with people having identities, but remember, that means the equity doesn't transfer as simply.

Finally, brands are complex, not one-dimensional. Don't try to be a one-note experience. Madonna has much more than one brand element. So does Guy Kawasaki. Don't whittle yourself down to a simple footnote. Be complex and colorful and interesting. Just be sure you can say what you're about in one easy sentence and that others have a sense of what you represent without your help. Madonna is a creative force of emotion. Guy Kawasaki is an innovator and experimenter.

64

Develop a Strong Personal Brand Online: Part 2

THE TECHNOLOGY OF BRANDS

My friend and interactive media strategist Adam Broitman[225] calls Google a "reputation management system." I love it. Essentially, Google knows what's true, as far as the uneducated are concerned. How does Google come to accept you as the authority on something? Here's how:

- *Inbound links from other sources.* If someone is linking to your web site, you must have information of value, especially if the person who's doing the linking is important.
- *Outbound links to quality material.* This is actually more for human love, but it certainly helps prove that you're a lively presence.
- *Readable, searchable pages.* If Google can tell what you're talking about at your web site, you are probably trying to offer something to the world.

---

[225]http://amediacirc.us/

- *Constantly updated content.* Google values freshness over staleness. (Don't we all?)
- *Listed in directories.* Google wants to know that you've submitted your site for inclusion in the more prominent search engines and web site directories.
- *Mechanical quality.* Google has a lot of other things it values, like well-written web sites that follow standards, and it takes a little bit of learning to understand them all. Hubspot makes a free Website Grader tool that would help you understand a bit.

That's what Google cares about, and that's how a lot of people are searching for you. But we do this for humans, because humans make the decisions. Let's look into what counts for your strong personal brand technologically, with humans in mind.

START WITH A HOME BASE

First and foremost, build a site to call your own. I recommend a blog, because a blog has the ability to command more attention from Google, on one hand, and because you can use it to build your voice, on the other hand. I recommend buying your own name as a domain (check out the list of domain registration coupon codes[226] for GoDaddy.com). It might not be your home base or part of your largest plan, but buy it now while you can. Then, if you have another brand that you want to promote as

---

[226]www.fatwallet.com/forums/hot-deals/725207

your big number one brand, buy that domain name, too, and put up a blog.

The aesthetics of your blog and your blog design are up to you. Pretty blogs don't hurt people's opinion of your work.

But we have to start thinking outside the blog, too. It's not *all* about you. Or maybe it is, but it's about how you get out and travel the Web, too.

BUILD A FEW ACCOUNTS

To participate on the Web these days requires that you build some accounts at various Web platforms. I call these *passport accounts*, because you need them to visit these virtual places. Here's a quick list of sites and why you should have an account there:

- Google Accounts—so you can use several dozen free applications by Google
- Yahoo! Accounts/Mail—so you can use several dozen free applications by Yahoo! and also take advantage of Yahoo's OpenID account
- Digg—social news site
- StumbleUpon—social news site
- YouTube—video-sharing site
- Flickr—video-sharing site
- Upcoming.org—social events calendar
- Del.icio.us—social bookmarking
- PayPal[227]—online money transfer

---

[227]http://paypal.com

- eBay—auction site
- Amazon.com—shopping site

This advice doesn't fit neatly into my bulleted list, but *take a few pictures of your head* to make avatars for accounts. Your company logo doesn't cut it with me. I want a picture of your face, so that I can identify you at conferences and the like.

SOCIAL NETWORKS TO CONSIDER

There are plenty of communities online, and these all have social networks to empower them. I could list about a hundred places where you might choose to spend your time, but here are some real baseline social networks where your presence might help further develop your brand:

- Twitter. If you don't "get it" right away, that's okay. The learning curve is about 30 days before you feel as though it's indispensable.
- Facebook. I use Facebook as an outpost, where I build my profile, link back to my site, and give people a bit more understanding of who I am and what matters to me.
- LinkedIn. This is a professional network. Don't let the "looks like a resume" appearance fool you. Write your profile as though a human will actually read it. Be interesting. Participate with the community, and you'll develop more awareness and build a stronger future.
- And a specialized network. If you have a niche or genre of interest, be sure to find a vibrant community to join

that surrounds it. Love photography? Get into Flickr. Huge on music? Get into Blip.fm or Pandora.com or any of a million other cool music communities.

The change from the first Web to the new Web is that you have to be where the people are. It's not as much about your site as it is about your ability to participate where conversations are being held.

100 Personal Branding Tactics Using Social Media

You are not special. You are not a beautiful or unique snowflake. You are the same decaying organic matter as everything else.
— Tyler Durden, Fight Club

Branding oneself in an online environment built on entropy and go-baby-go is difficult at best, and impossible if you forget to take your happy pills. To that end, I've come up with a quick list of 100 things you might do to help with these efforts. Feel free to add your ideas to the comments section of my blog at http://chrisbrogan.com/comments-from-101.

If you like this one, please don't hesitate to Stumble, blog, Digg, bookmark, and otherwise promote this list. That's another tactic, by the way.

LISTENING

- Build ego searches using Technorati and Google Blog Search.
- Comment frequently (and meaningfully) on blogs that write about you and your posts.
- Don't forget the conversations hiding in Twitter (use Summize.com) and FriendFeed. Be sure to stay aware of those.
- If you can afford it, buy professional listening tools, like Radian6 or others in that category.
- Use Google Reader to store your ego searches.
- Use Yahoo! Site Explorer to see who's linking to your site.
- Use heat map tools like CrazyEgg to see how people relate to your site.
- Listen to others in your area of expertise. Learn from them.
- Listen to thought leaders in other areas, and see how their ideas apply to you.
- Don't forget podcasts. Check out iTunes and see who's talking about your area of interest.
- Track things like audience/community sentiment (positive/negative) if you want to map effort to results.

HOME BASE

- Home base is your blog/website. Not everyone needs a blog. But most people who want to develop a personal brand do.

- Buy an easy-to-remember, easy-to-spell, content-appropriate domain name if you can. Don't be *TOO* clever.

- A really nice layout doesn't have to cost a lot, but shows you're more than a social media dabbler.

- Your "About" page should be about you *AND* your business, should the blog be professional in nature. At least, it should be about you.

- Make sure it's easy to comment on your site.

- Make sure it's easy for people to subscribe to your site's content.

- Use easy to read fonts and colors.

- A site laden with ads is a site that doesn't cherish its audience. Be thoughtful.

- Pay attention to which widgets you use in your sidebar. Don't be frivolous.

- Load time is key. Test your blog when you make changes to ensure your load times are reasonable.

- Register your site with all the top search engines.

- Claim your site on Technorati.com.

- Use Website Grader to make sure your site is well built in Google's eyes.

PASSPORTS

- Passports are accounts on other social networks and social media platforms. It's a good idea to build an account on some of these sites to further extend your personal branding.
- Twitter.com is a must if you have a social media audience. It also connects you to other practitioners.
- Facebook and/or MySpace are useful social networks where you can build outposts (see next list).
- Get a Flickr account for photo sharing.
- Get a YouTube account for video uploading.
- Get a StumbleUpon.com account for voting.
- Get a Digg.com account for voting, as well.
- Get an Upcoming.org account to promote events.
- Get a Del.icio.us account for social bookmarking.
- Get a WordPress.com account for its OpenID benefits.
- Get a LinkedIn account for your professional network.
- Get a Plaxo accout for contact management.
- Get a Gmail.com account for use with reader, calendar, docs, and more.

OUTPOSTS

- Build RSS outposts on Facebook. Add Flog Blog and several other RSS tools.
- Build a similar outpost on MySpace, if your audience might be there.

- Make sure your social media is listed in your LinkedIn profile.
- Add a link to your blog in your e-mail signature file (this is still an outpost).
- Be sure your social network profile on all sites has your blog listed, no matter where you have to put it to list it.
- Make sure your passport accounts (see previous list) point to your blog and sites.
- Use social networks respectfully to share the best of your content in a community-appropriate setting.
- Don't forget places like Yahoo! Groups, Craigslist, and online forums.
- An e-mail newsletter with some links to your blog makes for an effective outpost, especially if your audience isn't especially blog-savvy.
- Podcast content can have links to your URL and might draw awareness back to your content, too.

CONTENT

- Create new content regularly—if not daily, then at least three times a week.
- The more others can use your content, the more they will adopt it.
- Write brief pieces with lots of visual breaks that allow people to absorb content.
- Images draw people's attention. Try to add a graphic per post. (I'm not sure why this works, but it seems to add some level of attention.)

- Mix up the kinds of pieces you put on your site. A mix of interviews, how-to, news-type information, and more can help draw more attention.
- Limit the number of "me too" posts you do in any given month to no more than three. Be original, in other words.
- The occasional "list" post is usually very good for drawing attention.
- Write passionately, but be brief (unless you're writing a list of 100 tips).
- Consider adding audio and video to the mix. The occasional YouTube video with you as the star adds to your personal branding immensely, especially if you can manage to look comfortable.
- Brevity rules.

CONVERSATION

- Commenting on other people's blogs builds awareness fast.
- The more valuable your comments, the better they reflect on your ability and your character.
- Use your listening tools to stay active in pertinent discussions.
- Try not to brag, ever. Be humble. Not falsely so, but truly, because a lot of what we do isn't as important as saving lives.
- Ask questions with your blog posts. Defer to experts. Learn from the conversation.

- Be confident. Asking for external validation often is a sign of weakness.
- Good conversations can be across many blogs, with links to show the way.
- Try never to be too defensive. Don't be a pushover, but be aware of how you present yourself when defending.
- Disclose anything that might be questionable. *Anything—* and quickly!
- Don't delete critical blog comments. Delete only spam, abrasive language posts, and offensive material. (Have a blog comments policy handy, if you get into the deleting mode.)

COMMUNITY

- Remember that community and marketplace are two different things.
- Make your site and your efforts heavily about other people. It circles back.
- Make it easy for your community to reach you.
- Contribute to your community's blogs and projects.
- Thank people often for their time and attention.
- Celebrate important information in your community (e.g., birthdays).
- Be human. Always.
- Your community knows more than you. Ask them questions often.
- Apologize when you mess up. Be very sincere.

- Treat your community like gold. Never subject them to a third party of any kind without their consent.
- Knowing more about your competitors' communities is a useful thing, too. Learn who visits, why they visit, and how they interact.
- Measuring your efforts in building community grows your brand as a natural extension.

FACE-TO-FACE

- Have simple, useful, crisp business cards[228] to share. Always.
- Be confident in person.[229]
- Clothes and appearance *do* matter. Wish they didn't, but they do.
- Have a very brief introduction or elevator pitch and practice it often.
- Ask questions of people you meet. Get to know them.
- Don't seek business relationships right off the bat. Instead, seek areas of shared interest.
- Know when to walk away politely.
- Don't try to meet everyone in a room. Meet a half dozen or more great new people.
- Never doubt that you are worth it.
- If you're terribly shy, consider finding a "wingman" for events.

---

[228]http://tinyurl.com/67e28l
[229]www.chrisbrogan.com/be-sexier-in-person/

- Doing homework ahead of time (finding people's most recent blog posts, Googling them, etc.) helps you feel "in the know."

- Make eye contact. It's *much* more powerful than you know.

PROMOTION

- Use Digg, StumbleUpon, Del.icio.us, and Google Reader to drive awareness.

- Promote others more than you promote yourself.

- Bragging isn't useful to anyone other than your own ego.

- Linking and promoting others is a nice way to show you care about people.

- Don't Digg, Stumble, or link every single post. Save it for your very best.

- Another promotional tool: Be a guest blogger on other sites.

- Another promotion tool: Make videos on YouTube with URL links.

- Another promotion tool: Use the status sections of LinkedIn and Facebook.

- Try hard not to send too many self-promotional e-mails. Instead, wrap your self-promotion in something of value to others.

- Sometimes, just doing really good work is worthy of others promoting you. Try it.

There are so many ways to get to the finish line. These were ideas I collected over time that have worked in some ways and haven't in others. Try some. Try a few at a time. Your mileage may vary. In fact, it definitely will vary.

Blog Topics for Business-to-Business Customers

Writing for business-to-business (B2B) readers is only slightly different than writing for business-to-consumer (B2C) customers. If you think about it, in both cases, real human *people* read both kinds of posts, so they are, of necessity, similar. The differences come from what is covered and, sometimes, how it is covered. One reason it's tricky to write B2B content is that it's sometimes far more dry than a consumer post might be. But you don't *have* to be dry. Here are some ideas and topics.

IS YOUR CUSTOMER ONLINE?

Recently, I met a guy who sells shiny concrete polish. I'm not kidding. Should he be blogging? Sure, if his user base is online.

If you're to believe studies, I'd say there are lots of customers online whom we don't know are there. Check Technorati for your company, product, or general industry name. If you find other people discussing you, you might consider getting online and telling your own story, too.

10 SEXY HEADLINES YOU CAN USE TODAY

Okay, I won't really list 10 headlines, but the idea is inherent in the headline. Stealing a page out of Copyblogger's book, write headlines patterned after current consumer magazines. They draw our attention in grocery stores for a reason. Alter them to match your business needs. For example, with some minor manipulation, "Five summer makeover tips she needs to know" becomes "Five summer makeover tips your data center needs now." Easy, eh? Try it.

THINK HARD ABOUT THE CUSTOMER/USER

Often, B2B content is written to represent the company. Swell. Except your audience most likely consists of your customer base and prospects. To that end, write your posts with your customers' usage in mind. Think about what they will want to know, and how you can be useful. Some quick ideas:

- How-to posts on some of the trickier aspects of your product
- Little-known third-party products that work well with your product

- Product release road maps (if they're public), and what the customer gets with each iteration
- Funny internal bits about the products (I wonder if Will It Blend? started as an internal joke between engineers)
- People profiles from the company's staff, especially if they don't exactly relate to the product

WRITE ABOUT YOUR CUSTOMERS

Can you do case studies with your customers? Have you heard really interesting things about what they are doing, with or without your products? People love seeing their name in print. Why not write about some of your favorite customers and give them some love on your post? (Well, maybe you shouldn't call them your *favorites,* because your other customers might feel sad.)

SHARE THE BAD TIMES

This might be counterintuitive, but your business partners might occasionally appreciate knowing when something is going tough for you. I'll admit that this is tricky. Many parts of your business relationship aren't exactly fit for prime time, and sharing a weakness is delicate, but in the event of a public-facing product or service issue, it's probably better to get it out there than to sit on it. If you want best-in-class examples of handling public concerns, check out the work of Lionel Menchaca and team at Direct2Dell, the Dell computer blog.

RESPOND TO INDUSTRY INFORMATION AND TOPICAL NEWS

People are reading more than your blog site, and they probably like lots of other sites better than your blog. But do you know who loves you (or who should)? Google. The folks at Google love you just as much as the next person, even though they rank you based on your web site's search quality, your site freshness, and a dozen other things I won't talk about here.

To that end, blogging with topical information in mind sometimes sucks you into the Google search fans. If you're in telecommunications, why wouldn't you write about the new Apple iPhone, even if you are the competition? The changes that Apple and, by extension, AT&T, bring to the consumer space must touch you in some way. Look for stories in the mainstream news that might cross over with your B2B customers, and write the tangential article to match.

ASK QUESTIONS AND SOLICIT INPUT

Finally, make sure that you check in with your audience regularly on posts. Ask them if what you've written relates to their use of your product or service. Ask them what they'd like to hear more about. See what's on their minds. You might find that the conversations that start on your blog, even the negative ones, are enlightening, and you might find yourself getting information that will help you improve your product, service, or maybe the business itself. Be open to it. All of it.

What else might you want to consider? What questions does this raise for you as a B2B businessperson? If you're a consumer, tell me about a potential B2B blog that you *wish* someone were writing.

Write for your readers, but lead like a leader. Never let the community become bored because you're phoning it in. Be vigilant for that.

Starting a Social Media Strategy

Let's discuss the parts and premises of building a social media strategy. Remember that these are just some starting points. When I build strategy documents and plans with clients, we usually start in one small "need" corner, fashion a goal for that need, and then come up with the various paths that could get us there. Those paths are the arching strategies, and then we lay out tactics to fit those.

BEGIN WITH THE END IN MIND

Strategy isn't the goal. It's the path you plan to take to get there. So, let's lay out some goals, then talk through how to build a strategy to reach them. Here are a few sample goals. Feel free to add some to the comments at http://chrisbrogan.com/comments-from-101, if I don't cover yours.

- Increase customer base.
- Generate leads.
- Drive sales.
- Build awareness.
- Make money from your content.
- Establish thought leadership.
- Educate customers.
- Customer-source part of your product development.
- Reach new channels of customers.
- Improve internal communication.

QUESTIONS BEFORE THE STRATEGY

Before we go too far down any one path, we should ask some questions:

- Are your customers likely to be online? Note that lots of people are online these days, but maybe you have a product or service that isn't frequently purchased via the Web. What's your story?
- Are you ready to handle negativity? Platforms like blogs and videos allow for negative comments, and some company cultures aren't ready to engage with those opinions.
- How will you incorporate this into people's daily jobs?

- How will you measure results?
- How long are you willing to give it a try?
- What's your willingness to experiment, take risks, and adjust your plans?

The answers to these questions might tell you a bit about your business, whether or not you decide to go forward with building a strategy using social media tools. Remember, it's a lot easier *not* to listen to customers and, instead, just blast out your messages with no regard to how they're received.

STRATEGY STARTERS

If we're going to put a social media strategy into place, we need to align the path we're going to take, and develop it with an understanding of how to reach our goals. Where are we going? How are we going to get there? Let's get there. How do we know we've arrived? Simple, eh? Let's start with the "how."

- *Listening.* Implement at *least* a rudimentary listening platform. (Google "grow bigger ears" to see an easy, free platform to start out with.)
- *Communications.* Build a starting place to hold your conversations. By this, I mean a blogging platform.
- *Methods.* Determine the mix of content you intend to create, and build work flow around it.
- *Community.* Most social media strategies have to address community and how you will embrace the people you seek to gather around your business.

- *Neighbors.* Develop a plan to reach out to others in your community, to comment, and to share.
- *Outposts.* Develop social network outposts where you can communicate with other communities and also share the way back to your own platform.
- *Marketplace.* If your strategy involves making money, build a marketplace external to your community. Keep these separate.
- *Attention.* Learn how to build awareness and encourage relationships with the media you're making.

WHAT COMES NEXT

Strategies must tie in to the main business. You might or might not launch pilot programs, but your goals, your missions, the resources used, the integration of the entire project must tie in to the main business. Building icebergs that float away isn't the right way to implement social media in the company. Instead, think about how to use the project as a pilot that might sway everything down the road; build it with an "over there" flavor to start, and formulate a plan to make it "the main thing" and also a plan for "let's bury that mistake." All three types of plan points are important.

Social Media Strategy: The Planning Stage

In coming up with the elements of a plan, I found a few surprises. One, I hadn't considered having a trial phase or project as part of a strategy. Maybe there are elements that you're not ready to roll out against your main brand. You might want to test those in a less direct way. Another surprise was that I hadn't considered the training required for internal resources until I had a conversation with Cynthia Closkey.[230]

What follows is simply the list of elements to consider when building a social media strategy for your organization. I'm submitting it to you for consideration in the hope that you'll find it useful for your projects and so you can point out things I might have missed. Please note that every item here explodes into all kinds of subcategories and information. This is just the overview.

---

[230]http://mybrilliantmistakes.com/index.php

SOCIAL MEDIA STRATEGY: PLANNING

- *Research.* The internal social media evangelist looks at what might be possible (maybe by reading my stuff as a starting point).
- *Trial or full plan.* Decide whether you want a trial phase, perhaps not company-branded (e.g., Target stores doing an ice cream blog without any Target branding, just to try the culture of blogging).
- *Goals.* Without a clear understanding of your goals for the program, these steps are worthless.
- *Target audience.* Is this blog for customers, colleagues, coworkers, moms—who?
- *End state.* Once this project is running, what will improve within the company?
- *Resources—internal.* Who has the responsibility (fun?) of maintaining a community, creating content, being a good social media citizen?
- *Resources—external.* Do you hire consultants, advisers, analysts to help you launch? Do you outsource the entire platform, like American Express or Fast Search have done?
- *Integration points with existing ops structure.* If this is a tiny offshoot of its own, it won't live long. How do you tie in what this person's doing to the larger organization?
- *Input from team.* Once you have your plan, do you shop it around internally? If so, help people own it. Give your ideas handles, so people can take the ideas and make them their own.
- *Reporting structure.* Is the keeper of the social media project a different person than the creator's boss? Where

does the information that is gathered go? Who needs to know when something comes up?

- *Training.* This turns out to be an important step. How will you handle it?
- *Legal.* The project should be blessed at least once by legal. Thereafter, do you make every step of the way a legal hurdle to jump? I lean toward no, but your culture might say differently.

Again, there are lots of ways to arrive at the finish line. You can add in the parts you might also need to consider; you can remove the things you don't want to talk about. You can shape this to fit the various business types you have in mind.

Social Media Strategy: Aligning Goals and Measurements

Since starting a social media strategy[231] series, I've been working diligently on understanding what goes into the process.

---

[231]www.chrisbrogan.com/starting-a-social-media-strategy/

I'm building a framework that, when completed, should prove fairly useful. Along the way, I'll share some of what I'm learning, so that you can learn along with me and, hopefully, influence the end results with your thoughts and ideas. Now let's talk about goals, strategies, and measurements. We start with a specific goal from my company, go into another basic example, and then open the conversation to you.

YOU CAN'T HAVE STRATEGY WITHOUT FIRST HAVING GOALS

Strategy is essentially the diet, but the goal might be weight loss, muscle growth, cholesterol reduction, or allergy aversion. It's not one-size-fits all. Before you know which diet to start, you need to know the goal.

STRATEGY WITHOUT MEASUREMENT IS USELESS

If you're not *measuring* the effort to reach your goals (Katie Paine[232] will be so proud of me), how can you be sure you're getting there? Measuring the effectiveness of your efforts is vital to knowing you're making progress. Remember that diets (i.e., strategies) often need adjusting along the way. It's measurements that tell us this.

---

[232]http://kdpaine.blogs.com/

SAMPLE GOALS, STRATEGIES, AND MEASUREMENTS

Let's put some real information out here and talk about it. I use a few items that I worked up for my own company, New Marketing Labs.[233]

- Goal: Increase attendance at our live events.
- Strategy: Add Upcoming.org and Facebook events components; blog; invite local geek groups. Possibly purchase Facebook ads to test that, too, targeting regional. Craigslist?
- Measurements: Add a "Where did you hear about us?" field to the registration form.
- Measurements: Check link referral logs.

That's fairly straightforward. The only thing I'm missing is some kind of estimate on how much I think these efforts might increase attendance. Truth is, I'm not sure. Should I have a number in mind? I will put one down, but I have no idea how close my estimate will be.

Still, the process is there. I've identified a goal: "I want more people to attend our shows." I've laid out a few strategies: "Put info about our show in more places." And I have a few ideas how to measure: "Use online survey and Web links."

In reserve, I have "blogging" and two other strategies. But I want to lead with these and see whether they make a significant impact on their own.

---

[233]http://crosstechmedia.com/

OTHER GOALS, STRATEGIES, AND MEASUREMENTS

There are many other things a company might want to do, and other approaches. Let's list a few here, and then, if you have others you want to talk about, we can tackle them in the comments section at http://chrisbrogan.com/comments-from-101. Goal: Increase leads for my product/service.

- Strategy: Build blog traffic with appropriate links to product/service.
- Measurement: Link tracking.

Simple and straightforward, right? I think the strategy should go further. Remember, "If you blog it, they will come" is not exactly true. That's where people fall down fast. Instead, I'd add the following to the strategy area:

- Augment blog traffic by adding outposts (i.e., referral back to the blog via RSS) on Facebook, in appropriate forums, in LinkedIn, and in other pertinent online venues.
- Augment blog traffic by adding useful tools for your audience that might drive more visits to download (e.g., an e-book).
- Augment blog traffic by using social news sites such as Digg, Mixx, and StumbleUpon, where appropriate.

BY HAVING THREE KNOBS TO TURN

If you look at it, splitting out goal, strategy, and measurement means that you can look a little more closely at *why, how,* and *how effective* your social media efforts are. It's quite simple, yet powerful, to put this lens on what you're doing.

I get lots of e-mails asking me how to improve one's blog traffic. My first response, almost always, is "What's the goal with the added traffic?" People blogging casually or for entertainment purposes just want a higher number. But businesses are hoping that more traffic to the blog equals more sales, more engagement, more something-that-translates-into-more-business. In those cases, it's not always more blog traffic that wins the game. Sometimes, it's building more effective blog traffic, building more pertinent connectivity, building a stronger process flow to bring readers into your marketplace.

70

Writing E-Mail That Gets Answered

Writing e-mail[234] seems to be a recurring topic of mine. I receive about 600 messages a day at present, and most of these require an answer. Some e-mails get a faster response, and some take days. Here's the difference (plus a few more ideas).

---

[234]www.chrisbrogan.com/writing-more-effective-e-mail/

ONE DECISION PER E-MAIL

It seems counter to cutting down on e-mail to ask you to limit the decisions required in a message to one per e-mail, but I've seen it have the opposite effect. To make my point, think about choosing to go out to eat as an example: The first message is, "What day is good for you?" and the second message is, "What type of food do you like?" and the third message is, "Should we invite Jay, even though he laughs a lot and makes it hard to concentrate?" These three questions all require a certain level of decision making. The e-mail about which day (better solved by a phone call) is different from the one about what type of food, and both are different from the one about whether to invite Jay (also probably better solved by a phone call).

DON'T EVER SAY, "QUICK QUESTION"

I say this because what almost inevitably follows are five to nine paragraphs explaining *why* the question is being asked. It's as if lots of context is needed. It's almost always not. I've written to complete strangers and used fewer than 200 words to convey my needs and interests. In fact, I do that often.

Here's a quick question.

From: Chris Brogan
To: You
Subject: Will you register for PodCamp Boston 3?

I'd like for you to register for PodCamp Boston 3. It takes place July 19–20 at the Harvard Medical School. I think it will be the

most powerful and transformative experience you've had with media in a long time.
Please consider it: http://podcampboston3.eventbrite.com
Main PodCamp Boston site: http://podcampboston.org
Let me know if you have any questions,
—Chris

YOUR SIGNATURE FILE

I'm all for a slender signature file. I don't want much hanging there below your name. Some people use this for a vast advertising plateau. Remember, more than one call to action often equates to none. Pick where you want me to go.

Good: Ways to contact you online and offline (never presume your e-mail address is obvious, especially if your e-mail has been forwarded by others).
Good: Very brief descriptor of your title and company (if it's a business e-mail).
Good: Link to your primary blog or web site.
Bad: All kinds of marketing at the bottom.
Bad: Links to every social network where you belong.

That's my opinion, but if you want to form your own, pay attention to signature files over the next several days. See what you pay attention to—and what you overlook.

FOLLOWING UP

With the volume of e-mail I receive, some messages get overlooked for a duration of time. Some people follow up perfectly, thus ensuring that I will respond; others do something that will nearly guarantee that I don't respond to the second e-mail. Here's what's useful in a follow-up message:

- *Brevity*. I probably know I haven't responded to you, but your message might not be top of mind. Just seeing your name and the words "following up" in the body of the message over a forwarded copy of the last one you sent me will usually jar me into action.
- *Simple summary*. Maybe your last e-mail was huge and had lots of requirements to it. If you sum these into a few short sentences, it might get me to complete the work.
- *Reminder of deadlines*. Lots of us work on all kinds of things at the same time. My job in itself is challenging, so when you ask me for help with an interview or the like, a little reminder of when you need it usually gets me back on track (especially if you give me two or three days' notice before the deadline).

NOT JUST ME

With more and more people overwhelmed, I'm not writing these suggestions and advice to help myself, except insofar as I'm saying that I have the same problems as other people. You might see some advice in here that you wish others would do on *your* behalf. If so, great. Feel free to forward the information to your friends who need to follow this advice the most, with a loving and courteous message before the information.

WHAT ABOUT YOU?

What are your ideas for how to improve the state of your in-box? How might you convince people to write e-mails that will be answered faster?

71

Where I Learn Even More

Check out the great article[235] by Bill Rice cited here. I'm not a salesperson. Not even close. I can cop to being in "business development," but that just means "salesman who doesn't know how to close." And we know about closers, don't we?

Bill's advice: "Know when you are just shuffling things around, and get back to the fundamentals." It's perfect advice. I think what's best about it is that I can apply it to my use of social media tools.

---

[235]http://bettercloser.com/2008/06/26/do-you-recognize-the-7-early-warning-signs-of-not-having-a-sales-plan/

KNOW WHEN YOU'RE JUST SHUFFLING

- Are you editing your profiles and pictures on all your social sites? Is this really worth it?
- Are you reading Twitter just because you have nothing else to do?
- Are you signing up to the next shiny object . . . just because?
- Are you oversubscribed to blogs and podcasts?
- Are you just focusing on your stuff and not on the larger community?

GET BACK TO THE FUNDAMENTALS

- Keep a steady and established habit and pace.
- Be clear about your goals.
- Fish or cut bait, but not both.
- Do big work first.
- Stop whining (loved Bill's advice here).

See? I got that from a sales post. Where else could I find influence? Where else could *you*? Keep your eyes open for ways to apply learning from other fields to what you're doing. It will round out what you're doing, I promise. What do you think?

Read Bill's article for more ideas about sales, and think how they apply to you.

What Do *You* Think People Want from Your Site

Forever the thinker, Jeremiah Owyang posted about the future of corporate web sites.[236] He cites Kristie Connor and Christopher Smith, who won a contest for their efforts to describe such. It's a great question. I'd recommend reading Jeremiah's post and commenting on it, but if you want to talk about it more, it's a great question.

PEOPLE WANT INFORMATION

They do not want marketing. When I go to Staples.com, it's because I need a store locator, or the price of a USB drive. I don't mind being sold potential values and bargains related to the information I seek, but I sure don't want to hear a big marketing pitch about whatever you think the summer value plan is going to be.

---

[236]www.web-strategist.com/blog/2008/06/28/the-future-of-the-corporate-website-involves-people/

PEOPLE WANT SIMPLE

When I go to GM.com, I get three easy choices right off the bat: corporate info, vehicle info, and "experience GM" (whatever that is). That's not bad, because the site slots me pretty quickly, but the risk is that the site is static, and that means there are few reasons to return over and over again.

PEOPLE WANT CONNECTION

Want the real secret magic? People want to feel "seen." There are ways to do that. One is something we do all the time on blogs: We comment back. Another is through polite(!) use of cookies to remember that you like things set up a certain way when you are visiting.

Further, people would like to connect with the people at an organization, not just through forms and chutes, but in as many ways as they can conceive. Know who does this well? Sun. Go to http://blogs.sun.com, and you'll see that there are blogs to suit most every taste. That means there are conversations to be had at lots of levels. Cisco and some other great tech companies are doing it. Are retail and consumer companies ready for this?

Musicians Play for Tips: The Importance of Comments

As I am writing this book, more than 35,300 people receive my blog in their RSS readers (or via e-mail). Another 9,000 to 14,000 come to the site directly, depending on the day and the post. Add those up, and let's say that around 45,000 people come read my stuff daily.

If 1 percent of you commented, that'd be 450. (I'm bad at math. Did I do that right?) The average post on my blog gets a respectable 30 or so comments, but that's only a tiny fraction of the folks who get a copy of each post. This got me thinking about other great blogs that I love.

I read several hundred blog posts a day. I comment on maybe five or six. So I'm in there with you. I'm not commenting much, either. And yet, if I'm able to leave a decent and thoughtful comment, I know that the other person will appreciate it. Sometimes, it's a matter of time. If it's that, here are some other ways to help.

IF YOU DON'T HAVE TIME TO COMMENT

Bookmark the post in a social bookmarking site (so others might find it).

- Share it in Google Reader.
- "Like" it in FriendFeed.
- Stumble it in StumbleUpon.
- If it's *really* good, Digg it.
- Note it on Facebook.

You get the picture. If you enjoy something, but don't have the chance to comment due to time, another great way to be helpful is to move it along to others in your network. That's why there are social software tools to begin with: to facilitate that very experience.

I could probably list 100 blogs that deserve more comments without breaking a sweat. You probably could, too. One might even be yours.

Now that I'm thinking about this, how does Seth Godin know when he's hit one out of the park, because he has comments turned *off* (for his own reasons)? Del.icio.us? Links? Hmm. I love my comments. It's often better than the post, and it usually tells me when I've hit a mark.

50 Ways Marketers Can Use Social Media to Improve Their Marketing

Social media isn't always the right tool for the job. Not every company needs a blog. YouTube worked for Blendtec (Will It Blend?), but it might not work for your company. And yet, there's something to this. Recently I've spoken to four *huge* brands in America that are considering social media for one project or another, and there are many more out there working on the possibility of integrating these tools into their business needs. Here's a list of 50 ideas (in no particular order) to help move the conversation along. Note: I mix PR and marketing. They should get back together again.

1. Add social bookmark links to your most important web pages and/or blog posts to improve sharing.
2. Build blogs and teach conversational marketing and business relationship–building techniques.
3. For every video project purchased, ensure there's an embeddable Web version for improved sharing.

4. Learn how tagging and other metadata improve your ability to search and measure the spread of information.

5. Create informational podcasts about a product's overall space, not just the product.

6. Build community platforms around real communities of shared interest.

7. Help companies participate in existing social networks, and build relationships on their turf.

8. Check out Twitter as a way to show a company's personality. (Don't fabricate this.)

9. Couple your e-mail newsletter content with additional web site content on a blog for improved commenting.

10. Build sentiment measurements, and listen to the larger Web for how people are talking about your customers.

11. Learn which bloggers might care about your customers. Learn how to measure their influence.

12. Download the Social Media Press Release[237] (PDF) and decide which parts you want to use in your traditional press releases.

13. Try out a short series of audio podcasts or video podcasts as content marketing and see how they draw.

14. Build conversation maps for your customers using Technorati .com, Google Blog Search, Summize, and FriendFeed.

15. Experiment with Flickr and/or YouTube groups to build media for specific events. (Marvel Comics raised my impression of this with its Hulk statue[238] Flickr group.)

16. Recommend that your staff start personal blogs about their personal interests, and learn firsthand what it feels like, including managing comments, wanting promotion, and so forth.

---

[237]www.shiftcomm.com/downloads/smprtemplate.pdf

[238]www.flickr.com/photos/mikeoliveri/2616959344/

17. Map out an integrated project that incorporates a blog, use of commercial social networks, and a face-to-face event to build leads and drive awareness of a product.

18. Start a community group on Facebook or Ning or MySpace or LinkedIn around the space where your customers do business. For example, check out what Jeremiah Owyang[239] did for Hitachi Data Systems.

19. Experiment with the value of live video, such as Ustream.tv and Mogulus, or Qik on a cell phone.

20. Attend a conference dealing with social media such as New Media Expo, Blog World Expo, Inbound Marketing Summit (disclosure: I run this one with CrossTech Media), and dozens and dozens more.

21. Collect case studies of social media success stories. Tag them "socialmediacasestudy" in Del.icio.us.

22. Interview current social media practitioners. Look for bridges between your methods and theirs.

23. Explore distribution. Can you reach more potential buyers, users, and/or customers on social networks.

24. Don't forget early social sites like Yahoo! Groups and Craigslist. They still work remarkably well.

25. Search Summize.com for as much data as you can find in Twitter on your product, your competitors, your space.

26. Practice delivering quality content on your blogs, such that customers feel educated, equipped, and informed.

27. Consider the value of hiring a community manager. Could this role improve customer service? Could it improve customer retention? Could it promote through word of mouth?

28. Turn your blog into a mobile blog site with Mofuse. Free.

---

[239]http://redcouch.typepad.com/weblog/2006/12/jeremiah_owyang.html

29. Learn what other free tools might work for community building (e.g., MyBlogLog[240]).

30. Make sure you offer the basics on your site, such as an e-mail alternative to an RSS subscription. In fact, the more ways you can spread and distribute your content, the better.

31. Investigate whether your product sells better by recommendation or by education. Use either wikis or widgets to help recommend; use videos and podcasts for education.

32. Make WebsiteGrader.com your first stop for understanding the technical quality of a web site.

33. Make Compete.com your next stop for understanding a site's traffic. Then, mash it against competitors' sites.

34. Do *not* to ask for 40 pieces of demographic data when giving something away for free. Instead, collect little bits over time. Gently.

35. Remember that the people on social networks are all people, have likely been there a while, might know each other, and know that you're new. Tread gently into new territories. Don't *not* go. Just go gently.

36. Help customers and prospects connect with you simply on your various networks. Consider a Lijit Wijit or another aggregator widget.

37. Voting mechanisms like those used on Digg.com show your customers you care about which information is useful to them.

38. Track your inbound links, and when they come from blogs, be sure to comment on a few posts and build a relationship with the blogger.

39. Find a bunch of bloggers and podcasters whose work you admire, and ask them for opinions on your social media

---

[240]www.MyBlogLog.com

projects. See if you can give them a free sneak peek at something, or offer some other "you're special" reward for their time and effort (if it's material, ask them to disclose it).

40. Learn all you can about how *not* to pitch bloggers. Excellent resource: Susan Getgood.[241]

41. Try out shooting video interviews and video press releases and other bits of video to build more personable relationships. Don't throw out text, but try adding video.

42. Explore several viewpoints about social media marketing.[242]

43. Women are adding lots of value[243] to social media. Get to know the ones making a difference. (And check out BlogHer as an event to explore.)

44. Experiment with different lengths and forms of video. Is "entertaining and funny but brief" better than "longer but more informative"? Don't stop with one attempt. And try more than one hosting platform to test out features.

45. Work with practitioners and media makers to see how they can use their skills to solve your problems. Don't be afraid to set up pilot programs instead of diving in head first.

46. People power social media. Learn to believe in the value of people. Sounds hippie, but it's the key.

47. Spread good ideas far. Reblog them. Bookmark them. Vote them up at social sites. Be a good citizen.

48. Don't be afraid to fail. Be ready to apologize. Admit when you've made a mistake.

49. Reexamine who in the organization might benefit from your social media efforts. Help equip them to learn from your project.

---

[241]http://getgood.typepad.com/getgood_strategic_marketi/2008/07/batter-up-bad-p.html

[242]www.techipedia.com/2008/social-media-marketers/

[243]www.conversationalmediamarketing.com/

50. Use the same tools you're trying out externally for internal uses, if that makes sense, and learn about how this technology empowers your business collaboration, too.

Consider this a start. You probably could add another 50 tips for marketers and PR professionals to consider by adding to the comments section of my blog at http://chrisbrogan.com/comments-from-101 or by blogging an additional list at your site. I know you have some ideas that I've missed. Care to share?

75

Should Hotels Have Social Networks?

I think about this all the time. I want loosely joined social networks for those times when we have an opportunity to meet like-minded people. When I visited the famous Nikko hotel in San Francisco a few months back, I saw all kinds of interesting people in the lobby. At conferences, I'm always wondering who from the event might be staying at my hotel. I think there's something to it, but only if done right.

IDEAS FOR A HOTEL SOCIAL NETWORK

Here are some ideas. Could you think about this, too? What would you add?

- *Opt-in*. There *has* to be opt-in.
- *Levels of privacy*. Should have an anonymous e-mail washer similar to Craigslist, but then include options for revealing further info.
- *Monitoring*. I suppose legal restrictions and good community would require someone to watch the community.
- *Some kind of questionnaire*. I might want to be able to filter, like LinkedIn, the reasons why someone might want to reach me, and then decide what I'm up for—or not up for.

Seems like a start. What else?

WHAT NOT TO DO

I think there are some pitfalls to this, too. Lots of ways it could be implemented poorly.

- Don't require hefty registration processes. Make it easier than that. Perhaps only room number, e-mail address (validated), and then profile info and options.
- Advertising thinly would be okay, but too much wouldn't work nicely. Besides, this should be a $5 addition to your bill, similar to a movie rental.

- Don't push any kind of "singles" agenda. You don't want to become the hookup hotel. Um, unless you do.
- Don't allow third-party vending of that information.

SOME COOL THINGS

Okay, well, I think they're cool. What do you think?

- Text messaging arbitrage to allow for temporary text access to other opted-in guests for the duration (meaning you don't exchange cell numbers—as with Twitter).
- Potential for guest-organized collaboration. What if 14 musicians find out they are staying in the same place? Jam session?
- Green opportunities, such as ride sharing and/or recreational meetups.

Essential Skills of a Community Manager

Community manager is a role that more companies will adopt in the coming years. Jeremiah Owyang provides a huge list[244]

---

[244]www.web-strategist.com/blog/2008/06/20/list-of-social-computing-strategists-and-community-managers-for-large-corporations-2008/

of companies that have such a champion already, and, more recently, he gave businesses a scorecard[245] to determine whether start-ups should have a community manager.

I've talked about managing a community and what it takes. I've discussed what I want in a social media expert. I've even written about how we might do community management wrong. Here are some pieces of the puzzle that I think are vital to the role, and to its adoption for most businesses.

THE ESSENTIAL SKILLS OF A COMMUNITY MANAGER

The best community managers operate as a good party host mixed with a fine restaurant host. I make a distinction, because a party is more personal, and a restaurant requires its host to think with a business mind. Community managers need both skill sets in equal measure. A party host will connect people together, praise incoming guests appropriately, maintain conversations throughout the event, and see everyone safely off with a smile and a wave. A restaurant host must be certain the ambience is just right, know that the kitchen is functioning appropriately, and help the rest of the staff pull off a flawless dining experience. Blending these two mind-sets suits a company's community manager well.

Community managers must be experienced communicators. One thing a communicator needs to do well is *listen*. Part of that

---

[245]www.web-strategist.com/blog/2008/07/16/scorecard-should-startups-have-community-managers/

involves building sites and community spaces such that people have a place to engage you directly, and part of that means using listening tools to understand what's being said about you elsewhere. Upon hearing and understanding, community managers should engage with their own authentic voice, not with a marketing message.

Community managers are ambassadors and advocates in one. This is complex, but community managers owe their first responsibility to their employer, yet they must convey the voice of the people (customers and other stakeholders) such that the company fully understands the mood of the marketplace, the needs of the people, and the customers' intentions. Further, community managers must clearly understand the community's position in the marketplace and communicate it in such a way that customers don't feel they are being fed a line.

Community managers are bodyguards and protectors. Some communities find a bad apple in their midst. A solid community manager will understand the difference between a vocal critic and a curmudgeonly troll. Knowing when to remove someone politely and quickly from the party is important. The rest of your guests will appreciate this. Just be sure that you know the difference.

Community managers must build actionable reports. It's not good enough to send e-mails to your leadership saying, "We had 54 comments on that last blog post." Metrics and reports appropriate to your organization are necessary to weigh the value of these efforts. Understanding the goals of your organization's use of social media, especially the relationship marketing expressed by having a community manager position in the first place, is the key to understanding what to measure. (I've communicated several measurements to companies over the past few months, each one reasonably different.)

Community managers cultivate internal teams for further support. Because community managers are the face (or at least *a* face) of the organization to your online customers, being sure to promote internal champions, leaders, and other teammates becomes important. One reason is that you want your customers and stakeholders to realize the humanity within the company. Another reason is more for the company's benefit: Should the community manager leave the organization, some level of continuity might be salvaged.

50 Steps to Establishing a Consistent Social Media Practice

You've told the boss that you're going to implement social media stuff for your organization, and in your mind, you've decided that means an account on Twitter and a blog. Maybe there's a bit more to it than that. For instance, what are your goals? Are you there to show customers and prospective new customers that you care? Are you there to solve customer issues? Are you building awareness and attempting new forms of digital marketing? Knowing this up front makes a world of difference.

In the meantime, here are some things you might consider when it comes time to implement your social media practice. Included are ideas for starting out, for augmenting your efforts, for writing content, for next steps, and for using metrics.

1. If you're blogging, make that a home base for all your other efforts.
2. Reread the "Passports" section of this book, and use it to think about your blog promotion efforts.
3. Pick three social networks to join based on where your customers might be. Three might sound like too few, but it probably will be too many.
4. On those networks and on your passport accounts, make sure you link everything back to the blog.
5. Get a second (maybe even a third) person in the company to build accounts on these places. Nice to have backups, in case you get busy.
6. Build an editorial calendar to think about your posting schedule and subject matter.
7. Subscribe to 50 or more blogs in a similar space as yours, including competitors and any industry blogs.
8. On all your presence points, be human, and write a human-sounding profile. Use a humanlike profile picture. (Did I mention *human*?)

9. After you've written your first blog post, take some time to comment on some of those 50 blogs, but *not* about your first post.

10. Set up a few searches as explained in 100 personal branding tactics in this book.

11. Make sure it's easy for people to subscribe to your blog, via a reader and also via e-mail. (Over 50 percent of my blog subscribers are receiving www.chrisbrogan.com in e-mail).

12. Run periodic checks of your blog/site using Website Grader to see whether you're technically sound and findable.

13. Use tagging and other metadata to improve your blog's search features. Most newer blog software has this built in. If not, look for plug-ins.

14. For whatever reason, graphics in posts improve audience. Check out Flickr's Creative Commons pool to learn how to use of graphics appropriately.

15. Consider a nice, clean theme for your blog's design. There are many free themes for different blogs, and some inexpensive ones, like Thesis,[246] that are worth every penny.

16. Outside of your blog, be sure to update/refresh the information on your social networks every two or three weeks. *Use* the networks more often, but refresh your profiles and other info.

17. Seek out opportunities to guest-post on more popular blogs in your space. Don't be spammy and overlink to your own site/posts. Add value.

18. On social networks, look for ways to contribute, even when they're not directly related to your company or product.

19. Continue building relationships beyond your specific need. Don't try to build relationships *only* with customers, for example.

---

[246] http://diythemes.com/?a_aid=t4ag3

20. Remember that social networks are a great place to look for hiring prospects, competitors, and so forth.

21. To create consistent content, read daily, and not just within your industry. Skim, synthesize, and post.

22. Use notepad or Evernote[247] files to jot down post ideas when you don't have a moment to write. Return frequently.

23. Riff off other blog posts you like, and add some value beyond linking back to those original posts (*and* always link back to those posts).

24. Go to the grocery store newsstand and find popular magazines. Pattern blog post titles for your field on their headlines. (Hat tip to Brian Clark, who taught me this.)

25. Skim news aggregator sites like Reddit[248] or Digg (or whatever's appropriate to your industry), and create posts from there.

26. Ask your audience what they need, what they're struggling with.

27. Revisit a month of posts and see what you've covered the least.

28. Think about things your customers, stakeholders, and/or prospects might need, and write about that, even if it's a bit off-topic.

29. Check your stats to see what people are searching for, and address it.

30. Use the blog topics posts[249] cited here for inspiration.

---

[247]www.evernote.com

[248]http://Reddit.com

[249]www.chrisbrogan.com/100-blog-topics-i-hope-you-write/
www.chrisbrogan.com/50-blog-topics-marketers-could-write-for-their-companies/
www.chrisbrogan.com/blog-topics-for-business-to-business-customers/
www.chrisbrogan.com/keeping-the-blogging-fires-burning/

31. Look into creating additional materials, such as an e-book or an online course, from your best materials.
32. Branch out your blogging into video and audio where appropriate.
33. Look into building a community platform around your content platform.
34. Invite your audience to guest-post where appropriate.
35. Add social bookmarking plug-ins, such as Add This, to your blog to improve distribution.
36. Look for cross-promotional opportunities for like-minded blogs in your space.
37. Consider starting groups on your social networks (such as a Facebook group) to further discuss the space you're covering.
38. Remember to comment on other people's blogs frequently, and show your participation in the communities where you have presence.
39. Occasionally, produce PDF versions of your better posts and e-mail them to customers and prospects to encourage growing your audience.
40. Consider a conversion engine, such as a free offer to help sort prospects from fans and audience.
41. Move toward measurements quickly, as this is often a deciding factor for companies to buy in to social media.
42. Create a simple report to show how you will report what you're doing for upper management.
43. Work out which numbers might matter. Comments received? Links in? Times bookmarked?
44. Rank each blog post on effectiveness based on your own criteria. Review weekly and monthly.
45. Figure out a downstream metric that drives real business value. Reduce costs to call center? Sales leads?

46. Never count number of friends or number of followers as a valuable metric. Separate quantity from quality.

47. As soon as you can, find ways to tie your numbers to marketing and sales numbers where appropriate.

48. Move to automate the numbers-collection parts early. Keep the sentiment-reporting parts human.

49. Set three-month goals to review progress with upper management. Determine whether this is having any impact.

50. Though these last 10 tips are about numbers, *never* treat people like numbers in social media.

Your mileage may vary, and some of this advice ranges from dead simple to overly simple. It will also require some customization, depending on your industry, goals, and interests. Consider it a starting point.

78

How to Reach and Influence Prospects

We talk about how social media like blogs and podcasts and social networks will help us grow our business, yet we are hampered in several ways. Some of our customers won't provide testimonials. Others will take a while to actually execute a project.

Still others have stumbled onto your site, and it's up to you to keep them. Let's talk about these prospects first.

WHO ARE YOUR PROSPECTS?

There are, of course, tons of ways to think about who your potential customers might be. David Meerman Scott[250] talks often about buyer personas as a way to better understand those you're hoping to reach. In my examples that follow, I've picked only three types of prospective new customers. You have many other people interacting with your media, and it's up to you to balance your efforts such that they align with the relationships you need.

Here are three prospect examples.

Private Customer

In the example cited here,[251] GirlPie's customers don't really want to refer her. This means she has a private customer. You could say that SEO and search marketing professionals often have private customers as well. In these cases, your audience doesn't want to tout your skills, because they don't want to admit their prior weakness, or they may have other reasons to stay quiet.

Newcomer Customer

Some of us have customers from larger companies who are very new. They've been tasked with adopting an online strategy, or

---

[250]www.webinknow.com/

[251]www.chrisbrogan.com/what-do-you-want-next/

a social media marketing plan, or something like this. These customers are browsing the Web, grazing through keynote searches, and hoping to gather enough information to convince their senior team that they understand enough to make some starter moves. This audience will recommend you, but only after they've launched their project (and sometimes that's a long while after you could have used their recommendation).

Clean Slate Customer

Several people find their way to your site by way of search. Perhaps you rank high in Google for blog topics (that's my constant number one search term), so someone searching for topics for their blog will land on your site and wonder what to do next. In this case, these potential customers might need a bit more content and guidance before they become actual prospects (and remember, we're talking *business* in this post, not community or other reasons for doing social media).

REACHING THESE PROSPECTS

In all three of the aforementioned cases, different tools will have a different impact. Here are some suggestions:

- *Private customers.* Consider an e-mail newsletter with discrete information that reinforces your benefits. In that newsletter, encourage forwarding. E-mail is much more intimate than a blog setting. Consider a private online pay forum that allows for anonymity, if that's also useful.

- *Newcomer customers.* Along with your media posts (blogs, podcasts, etc.), create specific-to-their-industry informational documents (or recordings or presentations), with an eye toward empowering your contacts with information that will convince their senior team to take action.

- *Clean slate customers.* In many ways, the simple answer here is to provide great content that's useful, evocative, and invites further inquiry. From there, if you see any responses that match your business offerings, reach out. Send an e-mail. There's no harm in exploring a potential business relationship, should you see signs that a person has a need you can help fulfill.

You'll note that I didn't mention social networks much in this instance. The way I use social networks is to build relationships. I do any business prospecting by way of the media I create. I'm on the networks to connect, to be helpful, and to learn new things. Hopefully, that distinction makes sense.

BUSINESS ISN'T EVIL

The social Web has enabled all kinds of new opportunities to communicate. Business and sales are just one portion of a large spectrum of ways we connect and transact. As with everything you and I talk about here, it comes down to clarity of purpose. If you're selling something, state it. If you're looking for customers, talk about it. If you're there to educate, that's fine, too. They're *your* tools. Use them the way you want. Just be clear and open about it.

What's your thinking on all this? Have I identified your prospect type here? If not, tell me in the comments at http://chrisbrogan.com/comments-from-101, and we can open the question to the community. What's your thinking?

How Content Marketing Will Shake the Tree

Some days, it feels like more and more people have abandoned their regular blogs and podcasts and have run off to tools like Twitter and FriendFeed. I just stopped by a friend's blog, worried that I had a bad RSS subscription, only to discover that he hadn't blogged since June. Another friend blogs only Twitter links now. What happened? Why are all the bloggers and podcasters going to Twitter or Seesmic or other temporal moment-in-time platforms?

One reason is that products like Twitter and Seesmic and Ustream.tv all give us even faster, simpler conversations. We don't have to synthesize information, compose a position, and build a post. Instead, we can talk back and forth about things we like. Another reason is that the feedback loop is so much tighter when doing a ping-pong game of ideas instead of the blogger-to-comments model.

But wow. I sure miss you bloggers and podcasters whom I know and love. Thanks to Mitch Joel,[252] Christopher S. Penn, Valeria Maltoni,[253] and a whole host of others who keep writing and/or recording something interesting and useful daily. To the rest of you, come back?

Write Your LinkedIn Profile for Your Future

I was speaking to one of the best upcoming tech bloggers[254] the other day about LinkedIn, and how I view it. To me, LinkedIn isn't a place to dump a snapshot of where you've been. It's an opportunity to stay connected to people, to demonstrate where you are now and where you plan to go next. To that end, I have a little advice for you to consider applying to your own profile.

---

[252] www.twistimage.com/blog

[253] www.conversationagent.com/

[254] http://shegeeks.net/

First Impressions

First, your headline matters. It's what people see when they accept your invitation, and it's probably the fastest first impression one receives. If you work for a company, put that name in the headline. When I don't see a company name, I wonder whether you're solo.

Your Summary

Here's where I think the most work can be done. When I look at my profile, I think it's a bit long, but I've done the following:

- Lead with what I do most.
- Lead with the type of business I want to do.
- Move into the reasons you'd like to do business with me.
- Move from there into all the nuances of what I do.

In every case within the summary, you should plan to write from the mind-set of the prospective employers (or clients), such that when they read it, they think, "I need to hire this person."

Tip: Refresh your summary every two weeks.

Your Work Experience

Here, I do something you might not expect. I make sure my past experience supports my current and future aspirations. I write the past work experience summary to highlight those functions I performed that will be useful to the current and future goals. Why? Because if you're still reading that far down my summary, you want to kick the tires a little on my experience.

Tip: Refresh your past work experience sections every four weeks or so.

Power Moves: Recommendations

Ask people for recommendations. Be smart about it, though. Ask people who can vouch for your abilities.

I receive a few requests each week for recommendations from people I know from Twitter. I'm sorry, but I can't really vouch for you. To me, the reputation engine part of LinkedIn is the most important part of the product. I will only recommend people I would hire myself or for whom I would work. Recommendations are powerful.

WHAT'S NEXT?

Here's a list of next steps:

1. Review your LinkedIn profile. Look at it as though you're a prospective new boss or client. Would you hire *you* to do something? If not, rewrite your profile. Keep it tight. Do as much editing as you can.
2. Enter your blog's RSS feed on the profile page. People want more color.
3. Add a photo. Not one of those weird grown-up versions of a school picture. Find a good candid. If you don't have one, go to a social media meetup. Someone will snap a good one

for you. Worried about discrimination? Guess what: They'll figure it out eventually. Get it out of the way up front.

4. Start writing quality recommendations for people you can vouch for. If they can do the same for you, ask for one back. If not, hold off. No sense making someone feel awkward.

5. Grow your network. LinkedIn and I don't agree on this. I say connect to anyone. It helps you build a network. (I recommend only people I can vouch for, and, to me, that's the point at which who you know or don't know really matters.)

6. Keep looking at your profile as it applies to your future.

Check out my LinkedIn profile. If you want to connect, I use LinkedIn.com/in/chrisbrogan as my address.

And you? What's worked well for you?

81

Consider a Marketing Funnel

Brian Carroll gave some interesting advice in an interview with Chris Coch at Information Technology Services Marketing Association (ITSMA). He talked about creating a marketing funnel, and how this differed from a sales funnel. In brief, his interview covered five points:

1. Create a marketing funnel.
2. Create a universal definition of a lead.
3. Use the phone.
4. Ask about goals—don't sell.
5. Define lead nurturing—and the right people to nurture.

Check out the full interview for more information.[255]

If we think about how this applies to social media, it's something we need to consider (somewhat) differently.

You might be blogging or podcasting for lead generation. If so, how are you helping sort your audience from your leads? If you're making media, that's a starting point to a conversation. Are you asking your audience about goals? If you need to further qualify a lead built from your online efforts, is the phone the next step, or are there steps in between?

The idea of a marketing funnel, where one builds up even more information and further distills prospective customers or clients from those simply enjoying the media, is something worth considering for your business. Have you looked at your media that way? How will you discern who's just consuming your media versus who's interested in doing business with you? What comes next after your blog post or video?

---

[255]www.itsma.com/NL/article.asp?ID=401

82
Content Networks and Storefronts

Back in May 2006, I wrote that content networks are the new blogs. With all kinds of great information out on the Web, I posited that people would start needing aggregations of content. Though many of us on the Web know how to roll our own collections of reading material, the general public doesn't want to go through all the work. Content networks cover more than just blog networks, and there are a few other ways to slice the pie than just thinking about blogs as ad platforms. Here are some quick thoughts about content networks and storefronts.

CONTENT NETWORKS

On one side of the equation are content networks. These include things like Weblogs, Inc., Gawker Media, and some of the other larger media creations. They include new offerings, such as Stowe Boyd's/Edgewards.[256] In a way, Alltop can be seen as a content network (though it is mostly an aggregator pointing

---

[256]www.stoweboyd.com/message/2008/08/announcing-edge.html

to the individual sites. Even I had a stab at it back in 2006, with the help of Kevin Kennedy-Spaien and Whitney Hoffman and Becky McCray and Megin Hatch and some others.

I continue to believe there are some great opportunities for content networks. I think that most of the models are trending toward ad platforms, and that's okay. It's what people know and understand, and people are making decent money doing it. Others are just gathering good stuff under the same banner so that others know where to find it. But there are other models.

STOREFRONTS

Another way to use content is to help people market a product. Some people use this as part of their effort to do affiliate marketing. For instance, there are review sites built essentially as a means to sell products. There are also coupon sites, blogs, and other Web platforms built just to sell things.

I believe there's an opportunity here for bloggers. I think that well-crafted custom content would be a much better way to sell products and services than typical ads. More than half of what Copyblogger and ProBlogger teach you pertains to being able to write great content.

There are a few ways to implement this. It could be toward the sale of products or services, such as an affiliate marketing model. There are many blogs that trade great content for potential affiliate sale revenue.

CONTENT MARKETING

Another model is as a lead-generation tool, such as what Corante[257] and Beeline Labs[258] have successfully executed several times. In those cases, the sale isn't direct and related to the site. It's more a matter of creating a marketing funnel, where there's a conversion point, and then the leads become actionable for business.

You could say that www.chrisbrogan.com follows the lead-generation model. I do get some business from my web site for New Marketing Labs or for speaking gigs. Mostly, I write to inform, share my explorations, and give you some potential new tools to consider.

I plan to investigate affiliate sales a bit more over the coming months, but not necessarily on my web site. In all cases, I think disclosure is what is most important when mixing a content site and a sales site. I don't think they go well together naturally.

DISCLOSURE: STILL THE IMPORTANT PART

It's a little tricky for bloggers. Are we disclosing our relationships? Are we spelling it out when we have a professional relationship with some product or service that we're talking about? Does your audience know your stance? Seth Godin posted his position[259] on this. I recently added a Disclosures[260] section at

---

[257] www.Corante.com

[258] www.Beeline Labs.com

[259] http://sethgodin.typepad.com/seths_blog/2008/08/policies-biases.html

[260] www.chrisbrogan.com/about

the bottom of my About web page, so that you'll know where my most likely biases are. (By the way, if I missed something that I should disclose there, just point it out and I'll add it.)

I believe that if you're blogging about how great a product is, *and* you're trying to sell some of that product, you might mention that relationship. In creating my Disclosures section on my About page, I opted to spell out the relationships I have with companies that have given me something to review.

In most cases, I've been lucky, because I've reviewed products that I really like, and I enjoy what they can do. When someone sends me something that I consider falls short of "all that and a bag of chips," then I'll have to be fair and honest in reporting that. That might upset a company, and it might cause a problem for the marketer who sent me the product, but if I *don't* do it that way, the negative impact is this: I'd be telling you about a product that I wouldn't endorse.

By the way, do you think all the products endorsed on TV are actually appreciated and used by the celebrities? I think we have an opportunity as bloggers to be a bit more open about it.

WHAT'S YOUR OPINION?

Content networks such as the ever-expanding TechCrunch and Giga Omni Media (GigaOM) empire are one thing. Storefronts such as FastForward[261] or DailyCandy,[262] which convert from content, are another.

---

[261] www.FastForwardblog.com

[262] www.DailyCandy.com

What do you think about either of these models? Do you see the benefits? Where are the risks?

How to Do More with Less Time

You need better time management. You're looking for time-saving tips. Whether you're in a huge organization, a team of 30, or a solo practitioner, it's fairly guaranteed that you have more work to do than you have time to complete it. Further, the effort it takes to keep up with people in social media and do it like a human being takes some time. In this chapter, I'll talk about how to do more with less time. Part of this will be about the philosophy behind it, and the next part will be about the tools.

MORE WITH LESS

I'm finding that there are two keys: (1) Have a simple system, and (2) automate everything you can. In both cases, this allows for more time to do the work that matters to you. Remember, a good chunk of our day is spent doing things that don't really pay us back (in any sense of the word). Part of this comes with a philosophical perspective to consider, and the other is pure business reasoning. Let's talk about the mind-set behind a simple system first.

HAVE A SIMPLE SYSTEM

I'm a lifelong fan of Dr. Stephen R. Covey's *7 Habits of Highly Effective People,* and also his later book, *The 8th Habit.* To that end, I work hard to begin with an end in mind. That helps me center on what I should be doing. For those of you who haven't read it, the point is essentially this: *The main thing is to keep the main thing the main thing.*

Sounds simple, but it's not. If you have big things to do and little things to do, focus on the bigger ones. If you fill your day with answering e-mail, your in-box will be empty but your important work won't be done.

If I were to sum up what I think about to keep my day flowing well, it's this: *What's going to move me closer toward my goals?* (My goals include company goals, personal goals, and family goals.)

Now, let's move on to the tools.

TOOLS TO AUTOMATE AND FREE UP MORE TIME

Once you have a sense of what you want to do with your time, you have to start guarding it. There are many opportunities in a given day when people will ask for some of your time. Distractions will chisel away at your time; and idle time will shift from a refreshing pause to a wallowing gap. Time is the one variable you can work with more than any other. Here are some ways to give yourself a bit more time.

AwayFind[263] is Jared Goralnick's tool to help you keep your less urgent e-mails at bay. I've been using it ever since going through Stever Robbins's You Are Not Your Inbox[264] program. Essentially, AwayFind lets you set up a small gate on your in-box. People receive an autoresponder message (you customize it) saying that you've received their mail and that you'll respond when you can; *however*, if it's something urgent, they can just click a link to fill out a quick form.

This gives me a way to tell people that I saw their e-mail come in, that I'll get right to them when I have a moment, and that they can alert me if it's something urgent. (By the way, four people have submitted via the "urgent" form simply to say, "I just sent you e-mail. Did you get it?" Not exactly urgent, so I tweaked my message to hopefully clean up that matter.)

Jott lets you call a number, record a brief voice message, and that message comes out in text format. You can import your contact book in there, and thus you can both send messages to yourself as reminders, and later retrieve the information. You can also send quick voice messages to others as text e-mails. It's a great way to get back some time while driving in the car.

Google Voice[265] is a voice-mail service that translates speech to text. I've been using it for months on my cell phone, and I'm *loving* what it does for me. I'm often in an area where I can't pick up my phone (meetings, webinars, etc.), but I can

---

[263] www.AwayFind.com

[264] www.YouAreNotYourInbox.com

[265] www.google.com/voice

usually scan a text reproduction of someone's voice message very quickly. I get back *lots* of time using Google Voice to cover my voice-mail messages.

Google Reader is my RSS reader of choice. I use it for reading blogs and news sources, and also for tracking social media information from other places. For example, Twitter Search has an RSS subscription button for the searches you cook up, so if you need to dashboard some social media activity, throwing it into a capable, fast-paced reader is important. I save lots of time reading blogs and scanning information rapidly through Google Reader.

Firefox is a fast, flexible, customizable Web browser. I use it more than any other application on my computer. To that end, I use it smartly as well. I use the tabs feature to keep up a few pages that I need throughout a day (my RSS reader, some search information, etc.). I also use all the keyboard shortcuts so that I can move even faster.

Evernote is a great tool for capturing snippets of information. It's a lot more powerful than that, including letting you snap photos and having a built-in optical character recognition system. It also has a mobile client for iPhone and Windows Mobile, a stand-alone client for Mac and Windows, and a Web sync. This saves me time in lots of ways, including making sure I have important notes at the ready wherever I am.

Also, use some kind of text replacement application. I use TextExpander[266] for the Mac all the time when typing. I have complete e-mails stored and at the ready in there, as well as all

---

[266]www.smileonmymac.com/textexpander

kinds of nifty HTML replacement information to help me with repetitive tasks.

If you can afford it, get a wireless cellular modem for your computer. I got one from work, and now I have no idea why I wasn't doing this all along.

WHAT I DO WITH ALL THIS

Giving you a list of applications and saying this will make your life better is like sending you a box of paint and wishing you well on your new portrait career. Let's go through a few ideas about how to do more with less time and how I use my philosophy, methods, and tools to do that:

- Guard your time. If you have work to do, ask yourself repeatedly if this work advances your main goals. Learn how to minimize the work that doesn't.
- Work toward checking e-mail less frequently in a day and also not being a slave to your phone. We forget all the time that these tools are supposed to be helpful, not constant distractions.
- One trick there: Kill notifier lights, buttons, sounds, and other indicators; instead, schedule a task on your calendar (or in whatever way you keep your appointments) to check your mail. (I haven't gotten that far yet, but I'm working on it.)
- Find pockets of idle time and use them for something productive. When I'm grocery shopping, I Jott little

audio reminders to myself about things to follow up on later. When I'm sitting in a waiting room, I read books on subject matter that nourishes my career. I use drive time for *lots* of things that you can do while driving.

- Build your projects to be modular, so that you can work on them when time comes up. Blog posts are a great example. I keep a text file where I can jot ideas for future posts. Then I go back and flesh those out from time to time (or delete them, if I can't remember what my notes meant).

- Learn polite ways to decline things. We say yes to *way* to many things. Learn very warm and polite ways to say no. (There's a great audio podcast by Stever Robbins[267] about saying no that I need to listen to often.)

- Decide how much of your downtime is really recharging you and whether some of it is just idling for idle's sake.

I know that some folks are going to retort that rest is important, that overworking oneself is a bad thing, and the like. You're absolutely right. All those things are true. I love relaxation and rest. I love finding time to rest and recharge, play with my kids, that kind of thing. My point is, if you need to find more time, there are ways to go about doing it.

---

[267]http://getitdone.quickanddirtytips.com/Saying-No-with-Honesty-Respect-and-Style.aspx

84

Creating Honest Content Marketing

Content marketing has an opportunity, should you decide to take it. Instead of going the route of old marketing, those who create content with the intent of building business relationships could try going the route of being honest, being genuine, being human. It's no more difficult than the alternative: crafting something that's dishonest but perhaps shinier. The thing is, if you start with honest and genuine, there's a chance that people will give you extra points for it in the long run.

In a recent post, Seth Godin offered some storytelling suggestions,[268] and the best of it is at the bottom of the post:

> Start with the truth. Identify the worldview of the people you need to reach. Describe the truth through their worldview. That's your story. When you overreach, you always fail. Not today, but sooner or later, the truth wins out. Negative or positive, the challenge isn't just to tell the truth. It's to tell truth that resonates.

---

[268]http://sethgodin.typepad.com/seths_blog/2008/08/creating-storie.html

In her post[269] about a series of viral videos created by OfficeMax, B. L. Ochman quotes Vinny Waren on how words become shifted one notch higher in marketing speak: ". . . funny becomes *hilarious*, and interesting becomes *fascinating*."

That's exactly where the troubles start.

Keith Burwell writes on his Better Closer blog about GM's employee discount pricing[270] program, and the fact that we all know this just means GM is not selling enough cars.

See a thread here?

Make your creations honest and open. Why not? It strikes me that most things would work better that way. Am I wrong?

85

How I Do It

When meeting people in a group for the first time, one question that comes up often is, "How do you find the time to do all that you do?" They're talking about the daily blog posts, the

---

[269]www.whatsnextblog.com/archives/2008/08/dear_agencies_you_cant_control_the_message_get_over_it.asp

[270]http://bettercloser.com/2008/08/20/when-it-comes-to-sales-strategy-dont-be-a-gm/

Twitter, the speaking at events, conversations, my actual job, and my family life. I often answer somewhat jokingly that I just type a lot. It's only *somewhat* jokingly. Part of it is typing. But I can share more.

Side note: It amuses me that people are always telling me that I seem very busy. (1) I am. (2) That's okay. It's a good thing. (3) Gandhi had the same number of hours in a day that I do. Time is never the answer. Learn to master your calendar, or it will master you.

DON'T SLEEP LATE

I have help in this department (children).

But I find that by sleeping no more than six hours (not recommended, but you asked!), I have a few more hours in the day.

DON'T WATCH TV

I don't have cable. I watch some movies, and I watch video stuff from the Internet in doses, but I don't have a TV habit. That gives me a few hours each day that some of you occupy in other ways.

THINK WHILE DOING OTHER THINGS

All day long, my head is formulating information. I'm thinking about things I've read and researched, things that I've learned through my own trial and error, and things I've gathered through conversations and other learning avenues. But my *processing* of that data goes on when I'm at the grocery store, or the gas station, or on my long commute. This gives me the opportunity to choose how I use the information I gather.

Sometimes, it's appropriate for work. For example, I have a newsletter (my job newsletter) deadline coming up, so I'm reading about emerging technology trends. But instead of just reading about them, when I'm standing in line, waiting for the man in front of me to finish arguing with the automated cash register, I'm wondering how Hewlett-Packard's acquisition of EDS further advances the mind-set of business processing over traditional IT computing.

READ GOOD PEOPLE

All day, I learn from people inside and outside my space. I use Google Reader to subscribe to lots of blogs from various interests. I read books daily, too, and often magazine articles. Reading and learning good stuff helps me come up with great stuff for my writing.

Oh, and I watch TED and Pop!Tech[271] and really clever stuff like that, too.

PRACTICE, AND TYPE A LOT

Want to know my secret to writing well? Write often. Write a lot. Read it aloud. Write even more. The more I type, the better I become at formulating my thoughts, the more easily my

---

[271]www.PopTech.com

language flows in a way that helps you read it, understand it, and find parts to act upon.

LABORATORY STUFF

Okay, for the bonus round, let me tell you about the whole thing, all in one place, in a way that you might understand it. Don't tell people. Shhh. Come closer.

Ultimately, I've come to believe that we are writing a new kind of code (like software, but also like genetics and also like secret code). This code requires human interface, which is *us,* but it's also the way we use our chosen tools and devices to convey information. What I am doing, more than anything else, is trying to use these tools, to master them, and to understand how this relates to human needs, human behavior, and how I might encourage behaviors to move in certain patterns that match my original intent.

Programming. I'm learning how to program, and to do that, I have to write lots of code.

Why? To be helpful. To know how to connect others. I met some *brilliant people* recently, and my first thought was, "How can I loop these people into the network, such that they can provide resources to others?"

Let me recap all that: I'm learning how to use these tools to build human networks, and then using what I've learned to help others achieve their business and organizational goals.

How? I don't sleep, and I type a lot. Right? Maybe that's all it is. You decide.

What I Want
PR and Marketing
Professionals
to Know

Since quite a number of people who swing by my blog are either in marketing or public relations, I want to address you, specifically, for a moment. I'm writing to you as part of this new version of media, as one blogger not paid to blog, not working for a newspaper or magazine outlet, not especially beholden to the traditions that have come before. I'm writing to you as a human being who likes people, community, innovation, and business, not to mention art, creativity, play, and many other things. I want to offer a few things for you to consider.

- Social media isn't that scary, but it is different from what you've been doing. For one thing, it's far messier and requires a lot more handholding.
- You have *so much* to gain from figuring out some of these tools and the way we're using them. And, contrary to typical businesses, most of us social media types are very willing to share what we know. Just ask.

- I love everyone who makes an effort to get to know me before they market something to me or pitch me. It works out so much better when you and I have talked, *without* the pitch, beforehand. And it takes only a few minutes every now and again to say hi.

- I'm tired of adjectives. Your new web site isn't *innovative*. The word doesn't mean anything to me anymore. Furthermore, let *me* decide whether it's innovative.

- Bloggers aren't all the same. I'm definitely not the same as Michael Arrington at TechCrunch. I'm not the same as Seth Godin. I'm not the same as most bloggers. I'm just doing my own thing, and they're doing theirs. It pays to understand which of us you're trying to reach and for what: Read the last 10 things we posted, just to get a sense of whether we're the right kind of people to write about your thing.

- Blogging isn't the same as releasing marketing materials.

- Putting up commercials on YouTube isn't video blogging.

- On social platforms like Twitter or Facebook, be human *first*. I know Lionel Menchaca as a human *and* as a Dell employee. You can do the same.

- Understanding Technorati and Google Blog Search and Summize goes a long way toward helping you listen and hear what people are saying about you, your client, and so on.

- You're doing great things here and there. Sometimes, you'll get praise for it. Other times, it might be overlooked. It's still great.

- Great things are erased quickly when you mess up.
- If you mess up, say you're sorry, *fast*. Acknowledge that you made a mistake, and then act on what you can do better next time.
- There are lots of things you can teach us media maker types, too. I learn lots from you every day. I do this through phone calls and by reading what you're sending me. It's a two-way street.

There. That's what I wanted to tell you.

Best Social Media Advice from chrisbrogan.com

I'm passionate about how certain strategies married to certain technologies allow individuals and companies to build things: reputation, trust, personal brand, community, relationships, and even marketplaces. My efforts to cover larger stories, tools, strategies, and more over the past several months have given you quite a bit to consider. But blogs are a tricky method for learning and reflecting. They're like a running stream, and if you step out for a moment, a certain point in the stream will pass you by.

To that end, I've made several lists of posts on my blog, www.chrisbrogan.com, grouped by category, that I think might be helpful to you. Peruse these at your leisure. Feel free to pick and choose the topics that matter to you. I hope this proves helpful.

There's a lot here. If you want to read more, sign up for my free newsletter, which has even *more* original content.) Thanks! With further ado, here are lists of blog posts that you can find at www.chrisbrogan.com.

COMMUNITY DEVELOPMENT

- Understanding Community Development Strategies
- Ways to Disrupt a Community
- Why Do Community Development
- Should Your Small Business Use Community Tools
- The Long Tail of Community
- If Communities Are Just Marketing Pools
- The Magic of Including People
- Meeting People at Events
- The Community Play
- The Community Ecosystem
- How Blogs Improve Customer Service and Product Development

SOCIAL NETWORKS

- Three Things LinkedIn Does Better than Facebook
- How I Use Facebook
- Things to Do on Facebook
- Facebook—Let Me See My Friends
- Fix Your Facebook Profile Now
- Facebook and the Social Graph—Who Benefits
- Five Things to Do on LinkedIn
- Considering Social Etiquette
- Social Networks are Your Local Pub
- Why Join Another Social Network?
- Marketers in a Social Network World
- Real, Live Human Social Networking
- Social in Real Space versus Social Networking
- Making Social Networks Work
- Improve Your Social Network
- The Importance of a Human Social Network
- Three Untapped Values of Social Networks
- Five Things to Do at a Social Networking Meetup

SOCIAL MEDIA

- Social Media Starter Pack
- My Social Media Toolkit
- A Sample Social Media Toolkit
- Participation—The Key to Social Media
- Social Media—Talk Is Cheap for Businesses
- How Big Companies Could Use Social Media

TWITTER

PERSONAL BRANDING

- Personal Branding and Social Media
- Passion Drives Personal Brand
- Elements of a Personal Brand
- Challenges of Social Media Types in the Workplace
- The Value of Networks
- Scaling Yourself

MAKING MEDIA

- Why Create Personal Media
- What's Your Social Media Strategy?
- Media Makers' Next Steps
- Blogging Advice for the Next Level
- Expand Your Audience
- The Future of Microcontent and Hyperlocal Media
- Why Bother Blogging, Podcasting, and Using Social Networks?
- Consider Your Media-as-Business Strategy
- Marketing Media Means Moments That Matter
- Using Social Sharing to Extend Your Message
- Performance and Your Audience—Blogging Tips
- Advice for Traditional and Local News Media
- Tagging and Metadata and Why Bother
- A Sunday Newspaper Strategy for Traditional Companies
- Promoting Your Media
- The Power of Links
- 20 Blogging Projects for You
- Succeeding in Independent Online Media

- Seven Blog Improvements You Can Make Today
- Keeping the Blogging Fires Burning
- 100 Blog Topics I Hope *You* Write
- 100 PodCamp Topics for You to Cover

I'm writing new stuff all the time at www.chrisbrogan.com. If you're reading this for the first time, please consider subscribing for free. If you're already a subscriber, don't forget to get the completely new and different content published at least twice a month in my newsletter. Thanks for your attention and time.

Special thanks to Alexa Scordato[272] for compiling this data on my behalf. It was a lot of work. Thanks!

---

[272]http://alexascordato.com/

Index

Entries followed by *n* indicate footnotes with URL.